Table of Contents

With wine & hope, anything is possible. (old Spanish proverb)

Dedication

This book and its pleasures are the happy bi-products of a remarkable mutual admiration society between cyclists and winemakers in France. It is dedicated to the noble labors of the latter (1 million strong) who make life much more interesting for the former.

Courtesy: The Wine Spectator,
San Francisco. Sept. 16, 1982.

c SPENCER '82

Grape Expeditions in France

Bicycle Tours of the Wine Country
2nd Edition

By Sally Taylor

Maps by Michele Brothers

Copyright 1986 by
Sally Taylor & Friends
1442 Willard Street
San Francisco CA 94117 USA
(415) 824-1563
(and 110 Blvd. Malesherbes, 75017 Paris, France)
ISBN 0-9604904-9-3
Printed in Hong Kong by Professional Printers (HK) Limited

Thanks to Friends

PATRICIA DUNN introduced me to France, on a bicycle, and to the wine country of Beaujolais. LENA EMMERY and CHUCK CANAPA joined me on the original legwork in the Loire, Bordeaux and Champagne regions. Lena's wisdom and expertise have contributed greatly to the success of both this book and Grape Expeditions in California, now in its fourth edition, which we co-author. NOREEN SHASKY is den mother and business manager at San Francisco headquarters.

In Paris, FIONA BEESTON and LUCIEN LEGRAND at Cave LeGrand, STEVEN SPURRIER at Caves Madelaine and the fine folks at S.O.P.E.X.A. have been patient wine and winery advisors.

FRANCIS KELSALL at the Maison du Velo has supplied major technical assistance. MICHELE BROTHERS drew up the elegant maps. Other friends have provided emotional support on both editions: ISABELLE BOLGERT, MOULOUD CHEKINI, ANNE CONWAY, LA CONTESSE DE GASQUET and her wonderful family, Ambassador DAVID MARSHALL, SEPP ROPELATO, ANN ADAMSON TAYLOR (my mother), and SUSAN TROCCOLO.

In Hong Kong, excellent production assistance from GALLEY PI, WORDS & ART and PROFESSIONAL PRINTERS have helped make this second edition a proper piece of work.

Thanks to you all, and to the many wineries of France who also participate.

— *Sally Adamson Taylor*
February 1986
Hong Kong

COVER PHOTO: In the Sauternes, by Sally Taylor.

BACK COVER: Courtesy S.O.P.E.X.A.

This book will fit in a handlebar bag.

BOOK DESIGN & MARGINAL RIDER by David Robinson, Words & Art, Hong Kong.

Starting Out

Herein we introduce the wonderful, bicyclable wine regions of France. There's no happier way to enjoy French country life and learn about French wines than from the seat of a bicycle. You've got the time to really discover the region, appreciate the sights and smells, stop often, and find your own meaning for all those names on all those labels.

As compactly as we can provide them, the logistics are included from camp grounds, to bed & breakfast country homes, to elegant chateau hotels; some truck stops, all three-star restaurants. Hills and winds are described and avoided where possible, viticultural (grape growing) details explained, and wineries recommended to contact and visit (just to get you started).

Six major wine regions, 12 tours, each 35 to 50 kilometers long: you can do the whole book in two or three weeks, with a car or a bicycle and train trips between regions. This covers all of France, but alas, not all of the French wine country. That takes a bit more time (and subsequent editions).

May the foods and the wines you discover be your lifelong friends. You'll be at home in wine shops and before a fancy wine list and if you cycle, you'll be one of the cognizant few whose legs aren't paté.

Lodging

This book includes the whole range of accommodations in France: from elegant chateaux where you can sleep under silk to local campsites where you can sleep under the stars. Only a few exceptional restaurants are mentioned, most in France are excellent.

The most exclusive (and expensive) places are marked (†) in the **DETAILS & CONTACTS** sections at the end of each tour. Make reservations for them in advance, using the Form Letters on pages 113 and 114. You can try them at the last minute, but good luck! There are other possibilities listed, including:

AJ, the *Auberge de Jeunesse* Youth Hostel system of France requires a Youth Hostel card and facilities vary, but the price is right.

BED & BREAKFAST *CHAMBRES D'HOTE*. The new French system of overnight lodging in country homes is a marvelous way to meet the French people and experience the country life of France. The hosts are casual and friendly and will not object to a short notice telephone call a day before your arrival. Prices range from 60 to 200 francs, depending on elegance. Most are around 100f for a single room. Breakfast may be 15f-20f extra. Some hosts also offer dinner with the family.

BIDETS: Many of the hotels of France don't have rooms with private bath. In some, you can pay extra for a shower; in others, you must do as the French do: use the bidet. That thing next to the sink in your room that sort of LOOKS like a toilet. Either sit down on it, facing the faucets, or, if you must, stand in the thing, fill your washcloth with warm soapy water and create your own "shower", letting the suds and rinse water run down your body into the bidet drain. The bowl, with the drain closed, makes an excellent laundry sink. DON'T use the bidet as a toilet. The WC will be just down the hall.

TELEPHONING in France requires 1 franc per unit of time. To dial long distance within France is not expensive, just have 20 francs in coins. From Paris, you must dial "16" in front of the 8-digit numbers given in this book. Otherwise, just dial the whole number.

Winery Contacts

French people adore their wine, and they adore the bicycle. *La Petite Reine*, the little queen, they call her, with innocent admiration. However, there are a things to keep in mind, when visiting the wine country *en velo*.

1)**CALL IN ADVANCE**. The winemakers are hardworking individuals often unable to accommodate unannounced visitors, even those on a *petite reine*. Places which advertise *vente directe* will be ready for drop-ins, though many close weekends and holidays. To be sure of catching them, it is best to call or have your hotel call for you, at least a day in advance. In a few cases, it's important to write ahead. Those are marked †. See page 113.

2) **TOURS & TASTINGS**. In each ride, one good overall tour and/or tasting is included that explains the winemaking techniques and the variety of wines of the region.

3) **BUYING WINE**. The normal etiquette in tasting is to buy at least one bottle when you taste, but you can't very well buy when touring by bicycle. Explain that you are *en velo*, but expect the occasional disappointed wineseller. Most of the recommended winerices in this book export wine to England and the USA. You might be a loyal buyer in the future, and most winesellers will cheerfully recognize that.

4) **SPEAK FRENCH**. It's amazing what bad French a Frenchman can understand, and what little English he will appreciate. Learn the numbers and the phrases of traveling life before you go. We give a bit of vocabulary here, as well as the *velo* named in parts. When you get stuck, go to the local tourist office, and ask them to arrange your hotel reservations and wine cellar visits. The more French you use, the happier and easier your trip will be.

La Petite Reine.

Food & Time

This book uses EUROPEAN TIME, from 0 to 24 hours. Just subtract 12, until you get used to it.

BREAKFAST will not usually be offered before 8 o'clock and it will be invariably be coffee *cafe* or tea *thé* and hot milk *au lait*, French bread *du pain*, butter *buerre* and jam *confiture*. The milk is your protein and the bread your carbohydrates, for the morning ride. Forget eggs and bacon until lunch.

Few shops open before 10, except the **POST OFFICE** *POSTE-TELECOMMUNICATIONS* which opens between 8 and 9, and does not close until 17 and 18. You can call anywhere in the world from the post office.

EVERYTHING (except the *poste* and the restaurants) will be closed between 12 and 14. If the weather is warm, come out of the sun for the hottest part of the day and enjoy the great French pastime of *dejeuner*. (If the weather is fair and you have distance to cover, the roads at lunchtime will be nearly deserted.)

Restaurants usually offer a **WHOLE MEAL** *MENU* at lunch that is good value. There is no bad food in the wine country of France. If you are a vegetarian, ask for a plate of vegetables *legumes* for your *entré*, all fresh and cooked skillfully. Don't expect lunch to be served graciously after 13:45 or dinner after 20:00 in the countryside.

Restaurants are among the best opportunities for sampling the local wines. If you can't drink a full bottle, get a *demi-pichet* of the house wine, usually local and most respectable.

Sometimes it's hard to **FIND A RESTAURANT**. Most small towns have at least a bar near the church square. Ask there for the nearest place to eat.

DINNER is not usually served before 18 hours...dark, in the country. Plan to reach your night's lodging in time to cycle out again for provisions, if no food is served there. The shops are open until 19.

IN AUGUST, virtually everybody who isn't enfeebled or eight-months pregnant in France takes their holidays, and many of them head for the wine country. Things will be hopping, and even campsites may be full.

France stops from noon to 15.

AOC/VDQS

The AOC *Appellations d'Origin Controllé* is a method of codifying established methods of growing grapes, of restricting grape varieties and annual yields, and of maintaining certain vinicultural (wine-making) techniques and alcoholic content. Started by the French in 1935 AOC or AC quality controls have been adopted in most of Europe's Common Market for many food products.

An *AOC* on a label of French wine means that the wine conforms to the peculiar characteristics of its region. The smaller the region, the more specific and stringent the AOC laws regarding the creation of the wine. Therefore, an AOC Brouilly will be more distinctive than an AOC Beaujolais, of which Brouilly is a small part.

The AOC wines account for 25% of France's total wine production. There are two more recent legal label designations: V.D.Q.S *Vins Delimite de Qualite Superieur* and *Vins de Pays*, but 70% of the juice is just good old *vin de table*. There are good wines to be found in all categories.

Great wine is an art and laws cannot make great wine. In a single day's ride, you will often pass through to several AOC regions. Watch the way the grapes grow, that will tell a lot about the way the wines taste. The density of the vineyards, the pruning techniques, the soil, the weather, all mean a great deal in wine-making, and you, gentle cyclist, have a front row seat.

Where there is no wine, there is no love. (Euripides said that)

Your *Velo* On The Trains

France is too big to bicycle between wine regions in the span of a fortnight's vacation, and a few mountainous and industrial areas make such endeavors uninspiring to most of us. Either drive or take the trains. Good connections tie all of France together by rail, but not all trains carry bicycles.

The French Railway guarantees to get your bicycle to your destination within 72-hours. Usually it comes within 18, and sometimes it takes the same train as you. Here is how to get you both there in the fastest time.

1. **BUY A TICKET**. Go to the ticket counter *billets* of the train station *gare* and buy a 2nd class (deuxieme classe) ticket to your destination, unreserved. (If you have a **EURAIL PASS**, skip step 1.)

2. **FIND THE RIGHT TRAIN**. Your bicycle is considered accompanying baggage. Go to the *Bagage* counter with your ticket (or Eurail Pass) and bicycle. Inquire about the trains to your destination that accept baggage. *"Quels trains a (destination) acceptent le bagage?"*. Those are the trains your bicycle and you can take together. Choose the one that suits you and register your bicycle at the *Bagage* counter at least an hour before it departs. It's always better to register your bicycle 24 hours before your departure, just to be on the safe side.

3. **TO REGISTER THE BICYCLE**. Fill out the two ticket forms (see sample). Pay 26 francs ($3) for registration, and hold on to your receipt, it represents your bicycle.

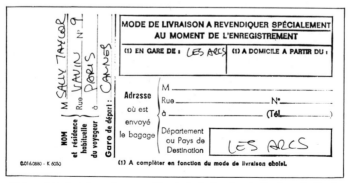

This registration form for your bicycle includes the destination, in the box, your address in France, on the side, and the rest can be left blank.

If you reserve a seat on the train, you won't know if you are coming or going.

4. **GIVE OVER THE BIKE**. Remove your bicycle bags, pump, water bottle and spare tube. Arrange your pannier packing so these things will fit together in a comfortable way, as you will have to haul everything around with you once your bicycle is registered *enregistré*.

5. You can get **INSURANCE** *assurance* for damage or loss of your bicycle on these outings. It's 10 francs per 1000 franc value (about $1 per $100 dollars), but unless you have a very expensive bike, it's not necessary. Security is excellent and damage is usually minor, and not worth filing a report form and repair estimate, in French. Repair service and bike parts in France are very reasonable. You are unlikely to have more than a few scratches, or a flat tire.

The trains are a funny combination of total efficiency (they are always on time) and total mystery (you never know exactly when your bicycle will reappear).

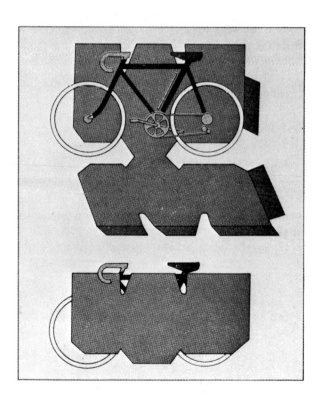

6. **THE SCRATCH RESISTOR**. Sometimes there are handy cardboard envelopes *carton du velo* to fold around your bicycle. They are just 10 francs extra, and great bicycle protection, but they are not always available. Ask at each station.

7. SMILES AND RESERVATIONS. Now that you know (or think you know) what train the bicycle is taking, you can make a reservation for yourself. This is not necessary, unless you are taking a TGV *Trains de Grande Vitesse*. Try to check the baggage car for your bicycle before you board. If, on arrival, your bicycle is not unloaded, don't despair. The mysteries of the baggage department are many. Your bike will be along in a few hours. Visit the *Maison du Vin* or *Comite Interprofessionnel* and get acquainted with the local wines.

8. OCCASIONALLY, especially on weekends, you can carry your bicycle onboard with you as *bagage a main*, without charge, between certain destinations. Most of these are the more localized destinations. We note this where possible, but the baggage czars dictate, so inquire as you go along.

9. THE PICK-UP. If you recognize your bicycle being unloaded from the train, you can pick it up right on the platform, by handing them your registration receipt. Otherwise, you'll have to go to the *bagage* counter. Between 12 and 14 hours, in smaller stations, everybody will be out for lunch. On weekends they may not work at all. (See "Eating & Hours".)

SELECTED TRAIN SCHEDULES in this book are subject to change. Consult your local station for updated *horaires*.

IS IT WORTH IT? Dealing with a bicycle on the trains requires patience and difficulties can tax international relations. If you are in a real hurry, go by car.

Don't forget to "compost" your train ticket in the orange machines in the station, before you board the train. It's not organic: it's part of the French honor system.

Renting a Bicycle

The French National Railway **SNCF** offers sturdy 10-speed bicycles to rent to some train stations in their *Train + Velo* program. With a 190 franc* security deposit, you get a reasonable day-tripper, a lady's or man's Peugeots with rear racks and lights. They are particularly useful if your bicycle doesn't show up on time at the station, or if you've come by car and would like to try a bit of cycling locally. They are not recommended for those with tender or sensitive seats, or for long distances.

The following stations on the tours in this book offer the Train + Velo rentals:

Tours (Tour 1)
Saumur (Tour 2)
Libourne (Tour 4)
Bordeaux-St. Jean (Tours 5-6)
Langon (Tour 6)
St. Rafael-Valescure (Tour 7)
Avignon (Tour 8)
Mâcon (Tour 9)
Beaune (Tour 10)
Chalon-sur-Sôane (Tour 10-11)
Dijon (Tour 11)
Epernay (Tour 12)

*Daily fees for the rentals: 33 francs/day or 25 francs/days (for 3-10 days) or 16 francs/day (for 11 days or more). You must return the bikes to the same station. *prices may increase

IN PARIS. Better 10-speeds, and even roof racks for transporting them, can be rented in Paris, if you decide against bringing or buying your own.

Paris Velo   Metro: Censier
2 rue du Fer Moulin   (Sundays)
75005 Paris   tel 43.37.59.22

The rates are higher than the SNCF, but the bicycle is yours until you return to Paris. The owner is a bit taciturn, but the bikes are good.

The Marginal Rider rents a Renault . . . . .

The "Details & Contacts"

TIME is noted in European hours, 1 to 24. Days and times in parentheses indicate days and times closed, e.g. (Sundays) means "closed Sundays". DISTANCE is in kilometers, 5/8ths of a mile.

TELEPHONE NUMBERS are written as they must be dialed, all eight digits if you are calling from anywhere inside France, except Paris, where you must dial "16" first for numbers outside Paris.

AJ is short for "Auberge de Jeunesse," the Youth Hostel system of France. CHAMBRE D'HOTE is the country Bed & Breakfast system. Both are explained on page 6. Addresses are given with the VILLAGE NAME in capital letters, as larger towns a few kilometers away may also appear in the postal address, and would lead you in the wrong direction.

The IGN is the Institute Geographique National, has an excellent _Series Vertes_ detailed (1 cm = 1 km) maps ideal for bicycle travel. You can buy them all over France, or in Paris, from IGN, 107, rue la Boetie, 75008, Paris, just off the Champs Elysee (Metro: Roosevelt). Better travel book stores in England and America also carry them.

The † symbol means this winery or hotel should be reserved or notified in advance. See page 113.

The text gives the names of villages to follow in sequence in BOLD FACE. (VILLAGES) in bold face in parentheses are those you will go towards, but not reach, turning off before you get there. Certainly, don't feel you have to follow the suggested routes. Take your IGN map and explore!

Although these rides are not mountainous, you'll want gearing in the 30s for carrying weight.

Oh, Those European Road Signs!
What Do They Mean?

This . . .   or   . . . This?

Man opening
umbrella

Road works ahead

Motorcycle stunt
driver ahead

All motor vehicles
prohibited

Tuning fork ahead

Dual road ends

You're about to
drive into the water

Dockside or river
bank

Parental guidance
suggested

Danger ahead

This space for rent

All vehicles
prohibited

(actual meaning on right)

How They Make Wine

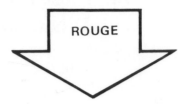

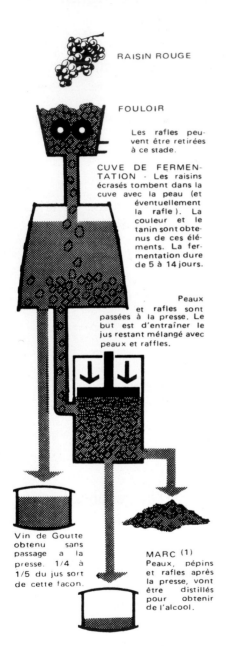

RAISIN ROUGE

FOULOIR

Les rafles peuvent être retirées à ce stade.

CUVE DE FERMENTATION - Les raisins écrasés tombent dans la cuve avec la peau (et éventuellement la rafle). La couleur et le tanin sont obtenus de ces éléments. La fermentation dure de 5 à 14 jours.

Peaux et rafles sont passées à la presse. Le but est d'entraîner le jus restant mélangé avec peaux et raffles.

Vin de Goutte obtenu sans passage a la presse. 1/4 à 1/5 du jus sort de cette facon.

MARC (1) Peaux, pépins et rafles après la presse, vont être distillés pour obtenir de l'alcool.

Vin de Presse
La qualité gustative du vin diminue avec le nombre de pressurage.

Red Wine

Whole red grapes are crushed and drop into a tank. The skins give color and tannin, and the *cuvee* ferments 5 to 13 days.

The free-run juice is siphoned off, and makes the best wine. The remaining juice, skins and seeds (about 4/5ths of the total) pass through the press. The *vin de press* diminishes in quality as it is more heavily extracted from the skins. The lees are used to make alcohol *marc*. Sometimes, the seeds are also pressed to make oil.
The juice goes into wood barrels for aging and is then bottled.

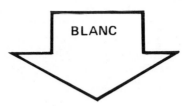

BLANC

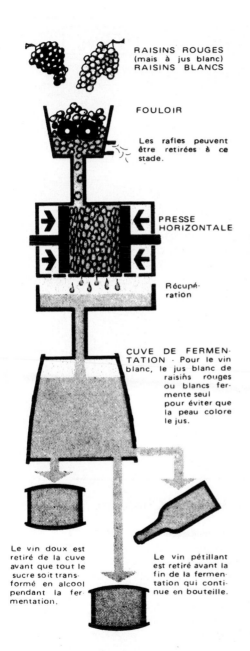

RAISINS ROUGES
(mais à jus blanc)
RAISINS BLANCS

FOULOIR

Les rafles peuvent
être retirées à ce
stade.

PRESSE
HORIZONTALE

Récupé-
ration

CUVE DE FERMEN-
TATION · Pour le vin
blanc, le jus blanc de
raisins rouges
ou blancs fer-
mente seul
pour éviter que
la peau colore
le jus.

Le vin doux est
retiré de la cuve
avant que tout le
sucre soit trans-
formé en alcool
pendant la fer-
mentation.

Le vin pétillant
est retiré avant la
fin de la fermen-
tation qui conti-
nue en bouteille.

Le vin sec est obtenu dans la cuve
lorsque la fermentation est com-
plètement terminée.

White wine

White grapes and red grapes with white
juice are pressed and pass through a
gentle, horizontal press, and the juice
fermented, usually at cool temperatures.

When the natural sugar in the wine has
all turned to alcohol, fermentation
stops. Sweet wine *vin doux* is removed
from the *cuvee* before fermentation is
complete, leaving some residual sugar.
Bubbles are produced for *petillant* when
the sweet wine is immediately bottled
and fermentation finishes in the bottle,
creating gas.

17

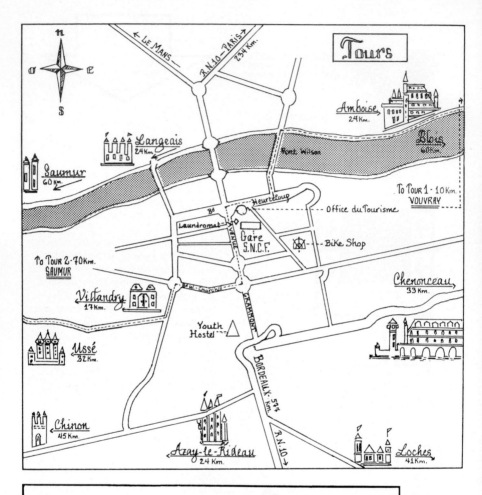

Distances from Vouvray to Famous Chateaux

Amboise et sa pagode	15 k.		Azay-le-Rideau	36 k.
Chaumont	30 »		Cinq-Mars	29 »
Blois	50 »		Rigny-Ussé	50 »
Chambord	55 »		Chinon	56 »
Cheverny	62 »		Langeais	35 »
Chenonceaux	30 »		Saumur	75 »
Tours	10 »		Loches	52 »
Villandry	27 »		Montrésor	67 »
Luynes	21 »			

White Wine in Three Versions 1

The Vouvray (AOC) region of the Touraine (AOC) wine area in the Loire Valley is famous for its slightly bubbly *petillant*, sparkling *mousseux* second only to Champagne, and beautifully aged still *tranquille* whites. Most growers offer dry *sec*, medium dry *demi-sec* and sweet *moelleux* versions of each, as well as robust reds. Good Saint Martin, in 380 A.D. built the monastery of Marmoutier at the gates of Tours and planted grapes in the nearby Vouvray.

The Loire is the longest river in France, has 3000 castles, and the wines reflect a combination of Celtic, Roman and Nordic influences.

Starting in **TOURS**, now a modern, well-organized city, with wide, open boulevards and well-preserved medieval architecture, don't miss the St. Gatien Cathedral and Old Town *veille ville*. The gastronomic heart of the Touraine; restaurants abound here. The train station *gare* is mannerly and the Tourist Office *Syndicat d'Initiative* is just outside, facing the street.

Just across the Loire and a bit upriver, is Vouvray, a day's easy circuit. The grapes allowed for Vouvray wines are known locally as *pineau de la Loire*, but are really chenin blanc, and grow best on the bluff above the river. It's a short, steep climb. The wines age beautiful in good years, as Ronsard and Balzac have given eloquent testimony.

The winemakers along the Loire rely on the unlimited storage capacity of the old limestone quarries cut into the banks of the river for 1000 years to build everything from castles to outhouses. Some of these caves still serve as dwellings, and are called (don't laugh) *troglodytes*.

The traffic is hectic from Tours across the Loire on PONT WILSON but then turn right, upriver along the N152. Two major arteries north quickly relieve the congestion and, in short order, the town of Vouvray and *La Maison du Vouvray* appear.

Sponsored by the local AOC winemakers, this *Maison du Vin* offers a good sampling opportunity. From **VOUVRAY**, take the smaller road, D46, which goes to **VERNOU** and **NOIZAY**, passing *vignerons* selling *ventes directes* and also pouring samples. The road is flat, along the rich riverbed. Turn left just beyond **LA BARDOUILLERE** and follow the valley towards **LES GATINIERES**, a small chateau bed & breakfast.

Climb up onto the plateau behind the chateau towards **LA VALLEE DE RAYE** and **CHANCAY**, small roads among the vines, on rolling terrain. Follow the small Brenne river towards **REUGNY**, turn left and climb again towards **LA LANDE**, following the signs to **VAUGONDY**, then **ROCHECORBON**. This route covers most of the Vouvray and if you descend at the **VALLEE COQUETTE**, you can taste at the wine cooperative before arriving back on the N152 towards TOURS.

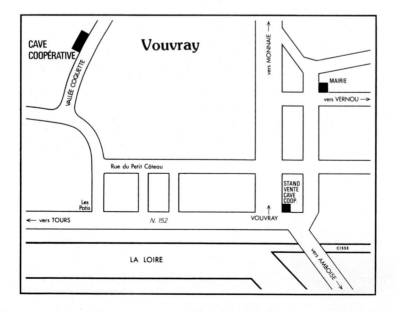

Selected Trains Paris — Tours (subject to change)

From Paris (Austerlitz)	09:06	10:15	13:36	17:15	19:23
To Tours	11:47	12:29	16:21	19:24	21:47
From Tours	08:54	16:30	17:07	18:48	19:39
To Paris (Austerlitz)	11:24	18:43	19:15	21:43	21:38

(Some trains require a change at St. Pierre des Corps, outside Tours)

TOURAINE   BOURGUEIL

TOURAINE AMBOISE   CHINON

TOURAINE MESLAND   VOUVRAY

TOURAINE AZAY-LE-RIDEAU   MONTLOUIS

SAINT-NICOLAS DE BOURGUEIL

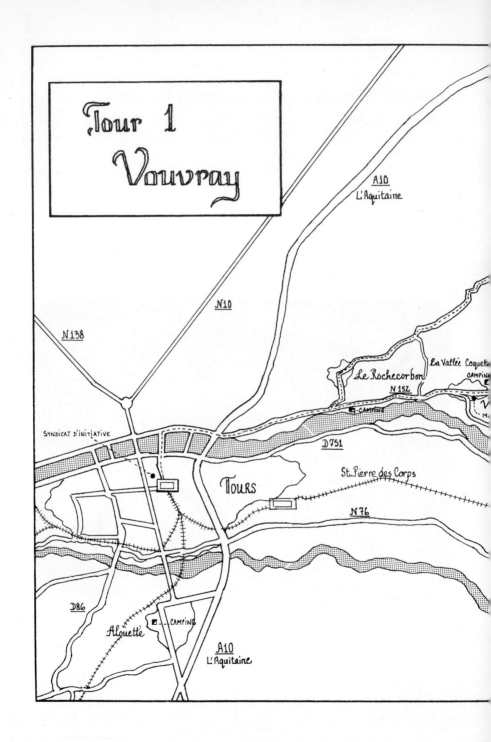

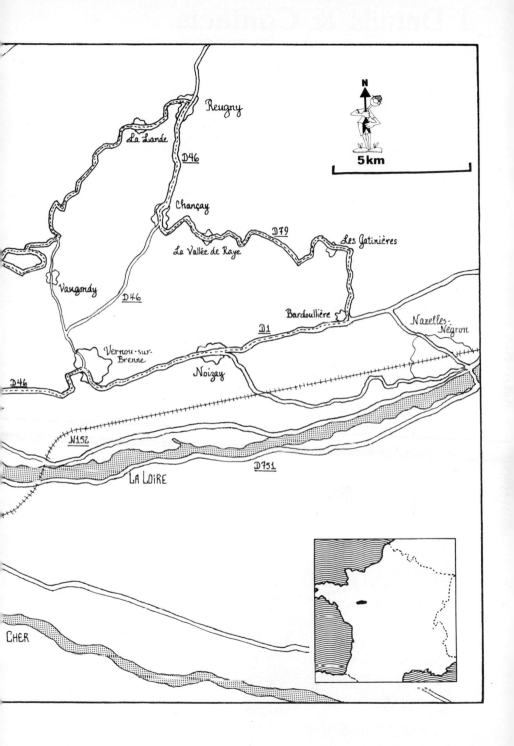

Reugny

La Lande

D46

Chançay

D79

Les Gatinières

La Vallée de Raye

Vaugondy

D46

Bardoullière

Nazelles-Négron

D1

Vernou-sur-Brenne

Noizay

D46

N152

D751

La Loire

Cher

N

5km

1 Details & Contacts

TERRAIN: Flat along the river, with 100-300 m. climbs up to the vineyard plateau, over the caves. IGN Map #26. Distance: 45 km.

AOC: TOURAINE, VOUVRAY.

GRAPES: Chenin blanc.

FOOD & LODGING: Auberge des Belles Rives, 76 quai de la Loire, ROCHECORBON 37210 Vouvray. 47.52.52.97. [†]
Hotel/Restaurant Bordeaux, 3 Place Marechal Leclerc, TOURS. 47.05.40.32.
Chateau de Beaulieu, Route de l'Epend, 37300 JOUE LES TOURS. 47.53.20.26. (4 km SW of Tours) [†]

Office de Tourisme, Place de la Gare, 37042 TOURS. 47.05.58.08.

CHAMBRES D'HOTE: Mme. Beatrice Sandrier, La Huberdiere, NAZELLES, 37400 Amboise. 47.57.39.32.
M. Etienne de Graeve, Le Clos-de-Cement, 37500 Chinon. 47.93.11.86.
Jean de Chenerilles, "Le Gerfaut", 37190 Azay-le-Rideau. 47.45.40.16.

CAMPING: Camping Municipal de Rochecorbon, 37210 Vouvray.
Camping Alouette, 40 bd. Chinon Joue, TOURS. 47.28.08.26. (On D751). Open all year.

AJ: Parc de Grandmont, 37000 Tours. 47.28.15.87. (12/14-1/16).

WINERY CONTACTS: C.I.V.T., M. Thevenet, Maison des Vins de Touraine, 19 Square P. Merimee, 37000 TOURS. 47.05.40.01. (Next to Musee du Vin.)
Ch. St.-Georges, ROCHECORBON, 37210 Vouvray. 47.52.50.72.
Manoir du Haut-Lieu, 37210 Vouvray. 47.52.78.87.
Clos de Petit-Mont, M. Daniel Allias, 37210 Vouvray. 47.52.70.66.
Cave Coop. de la Vallee Coquette, 37210 Vouvray. 47.52.75.03.
Clos Bandouin, Prince Ponhatowski, Vallee de la Neny, 37210 Vouvray. 47.52.71.02.
C. Pouperon, Vallee Coquette, 37210 Vouvray. 47.52.73.66.
La Maison du Vouvray, Vouvray. Open 9-19, (12-14).

BICYCLE: Rentals & Repairs: Au Col de Cynge, 46 rue de dr. Fournier, 37000 Tours. 47.56.00.37. Open 9-19:30, including Sunday! (12-13:30).

Clos du Petit-Mont, Vouvray.

I feast on wine and bread and what feasts they are. (Michaelangelo)

Saumur

Castles on Every Corner

From Tours, now, downriver on the south side of the Loire, pass some world-famous chateaux and more Touraine wines to another white and sparkling wine region, the Saumur (AOC) (pron. Sew-Meur). The sparkling wines are made in the "methode champenoise", but please don't call it "Champagne", the name reserved for the wines of Tour 12. For 100 years, the Saumur sparkling wines have won favor among the French. It's a pleasure to find out why.

The grapes used are Cabernet, Chenin blanc and Chardonnay. The soils are similar to those of Vouvray: a limestone base, with clay, then a shallow topsoil. The dry Touraine whites are best drunk young, when their fruit is full. The sparklers and the robust reds will keep.

If you bicycle from **TOURS**, take the D7 on the south bank past three major chateaux: Villandry and its gardens, Ussé the Sleeping Beauty castle, and Montsoreau. In contrast, one of France's largest nuclear power plants is at **AVOINE-CHINON**, then the ancient town of **CANDES**, where the legendary St. Martin, patron saint of wine, died. The old quarry caves are evident along the way, and several chateaux offer food & lodging.

It's about 60 km to **SAUMUR**, through the Touraine (AOC), Azay-le Rideau (AOC), Chinon (AOC) (Loire's best red wines) and Coteaux de Saumur (AOC) vineyards. There is frequent train service from Tours, on the north bank of the river.

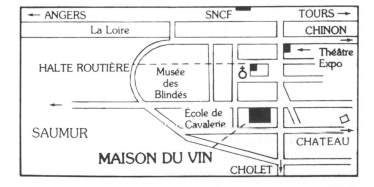

The town of **SAUMUR** might have been the model for Fantasyland. Picture-perfect out of medieval days, the 16th century castle is real and in excellent condition. Arriving by train from Tours at the *gare*, cross the river to the south bank. An island will obscure the view of the castle and town, that is the Ile d'Offard, where you'll find camping and a youth hostel.

Arriving by bicycle, on the south bank, turn left into town at the bridge, down a one-way *sens unique* street that looks like a pedestrian promenade, and is actually one-way against you. Follow the signs to the Tourist Information Center *Syndicat* and the *Maison du Vin*.

Continue straight out of town and west along the river to *ST. FLORENT/ST. HILAIRE* and the commercial heart of Saumur's wine industry. A half dozen major producers line the streets of this town, including Ackerman/Laurance, the oldest sparkling wine producer in the region. They offer a good tour and introduction to Saumur wines, featuring impressive quarry caves.

The vineyards are south and east of town, above the steep river bank on the undulating plain. The most impressive way to start on the *Route du Vin* that is signposted is to climb up to the **CASTLE AT SAUMUR**. This means backtracking into town. The steep climb puts you level with the vineyards and woodlands, which offer mushrooms in season.

From the castle, follow the *Route du Vin* past several *vente directe* south towards **CHAMPIGNY, ST. CYR EN BOURG** and the castle-town of **MONTREUIL-BELLAY**, returning to Saumur by way of **LE COUDRAY-MACOUARD** and **ARTANNES-SUR-THOUET**. These are lovely stone villages nearly unchanged from the Middle Ages.

The vineyards are pruned to the short Guyot method, without trellising. Chenin blanc is predominant for whites, with Chardonnay and some Sauvignon. Cabernet and Cabernet franc make the reds and rosé varieties. There are five different Saumur wines, of which the *mousseau* is just one: blanc, Cabernet rose, rouge and Coteau de Saumur.

Avoid the N147, busy with trucks and offering no shoulder. Stay in the old chateau bed & breakfast in Montreuil-Bellay, then return to Saumur to catch the train, or continue on to Anjou.

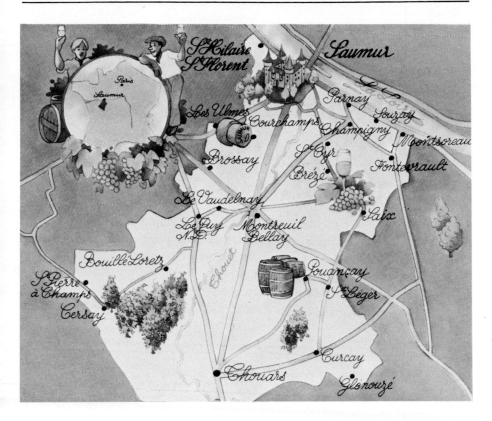

Répartition schématique des sols des côteaux de Touraine

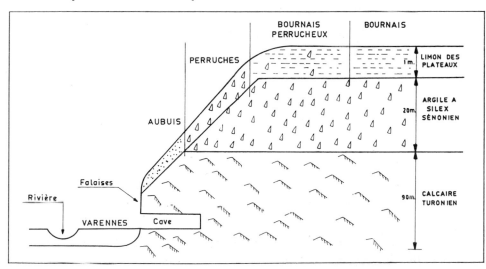

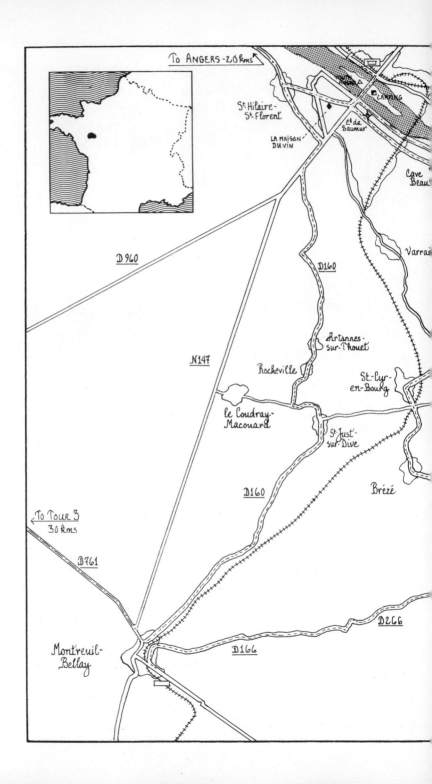

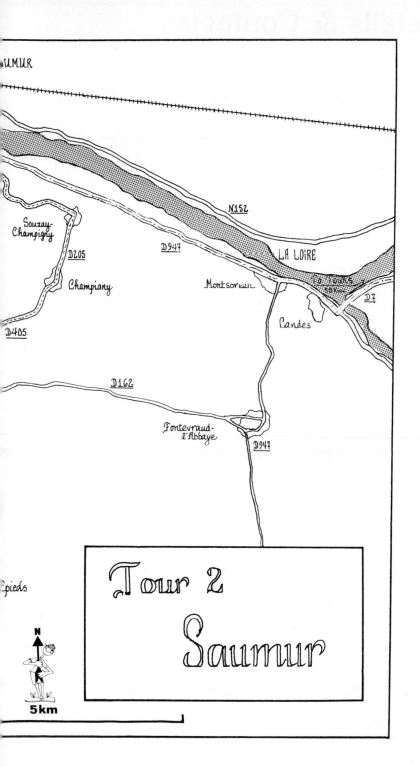

SUMUR

Souzay-Champigny

D205

Champigny

D405

N152

D947

LA LOIRE

Montsoreau

LA LOIRE 50km

D7

Candes

D162

Fontevraud-l'Abbaye

D947

Épieds

N

Tour 2

Saumur

5km

2 Details & Contacts

TERRAIN: Like Vouvray: flat along the river, a single climb up to the vineyard plateau. Wind out of the west. IGN #25. Distance: 45 km.

AOC: SAUMUR, SAUMUR ROUGE, SAUMUR BLANC, SAUMUR-CHAMPIGNY, COTEAUX DE SAUMUR.

GRAPES: Chenin blanc, Chardonnay, Cabernet, Cabernet franc, Sauvignon, Pineau d'aunis.

FOOD & LODGING: Chateau de Marcay, 37500 Chinon. 47.93.03.47. †.
Le Prieré, rue Traversac, CHENEHUTTE-LES-TUFFEAUX, 49350 Gennes. 41.50.15.31. †
Atelier Maridor, Mme. Priou, Quai Alex. Dumas, 49730 Montsoreaux. 41.51.75.33.

CHAMBRES D'HOTE: Chateau de Beaulieu, M. et Mme. Le Du, Route de Montsoreau, 49400 Saumur. 41.51.26.41.
Demeure des Petits Augustins, M. et Mme. Guezenec, 49260 Montreuil-Bellay. 41.52.33.88.
Dominique Dauge, "Mestre", 49590 Fontevraud. 41.51.75.87.

CAMPING: Camping le Sabot, rue du Stade, AZAY-LE-RIDEAU. 41.43.32.72. Adjacent to castle between Tours and Saumur on D. 751. (Oct.-Easter)
Camping les Nobis, Montreuil-Bellay. 41.52.33.66. North of town, near chateau. (Oct.-Easter)
Camp Municipal, rue de Verden, SAUMUR. 41.50.45.00. On Ile d'Offard, near Sports Stadium. Open all year.

AJ: Rue de Verden, Ile d'Offard, 49400 SAUMUR. 41.67.45.00. Open all year.

WINERY CONTACTS: Ackerman-Laurance, ST. HILAIRE-ST. FLORENT, 49416 Saumur. 41.50.25.33. Open all year.
Maison du Vin, 25 rue Beaurepaire, 49400 Saumur. 41.51.16.40.
Sylvain Mainfray, 63 rue Jean Jaures, 49401 Saumur. 41.51.31.31.

CHATEAUX HOURS: VILLANDRY: Gardens open 8-sunset; tours, 9-18 (Nov.-Easter)
USSÉ: 9-12, 14-18. (Nov. 5-Mar. 15).
MONTSOREAU: Tours, 10-12, 14-18. (Tues.; Mar. 1-15, Nov. 15-30).
SAUMUR: July-Sept. 15, 9-19, 20:30-22:30; April-June, Sept.-Oct., 9-11:45, 14-18; Nov.-Mar, 10-11:45, 2-5. (Tuesdays).
MONTREUIL-BELLAY: tours, July & Aug., 10-12, 15-19; Apr.-Jun., Sept.-Oct., 10-12, 14-18; (Mornings, Tuesdays in winter).

BICYCLE REPAIRS: Parts and service in the center of Saumur.

Jean Ackerman
(1788-1868)

Young Ackerman set out from Antwerp by horse to Reims to appraise its wines, the Champagues. He then went to the Loire region and fell in love with the daughter of his father's friend, Laurance. With his new vinicultural techniques, Saumur began to bubble. See page 113.

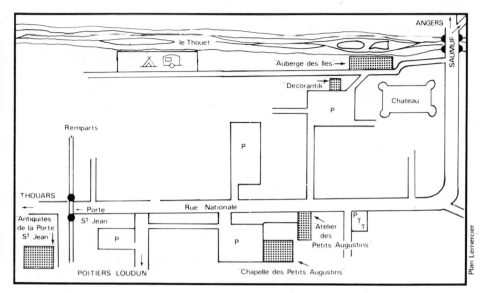

Montreuil-Bellay

Chateau Montreuil-Bellay, XII-XV c.

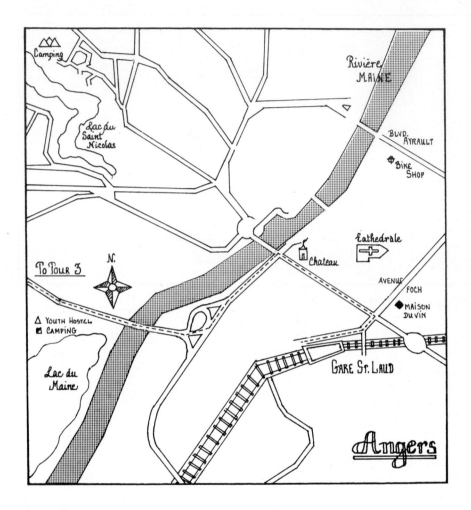

Anjou

A Sparkling Rosé of Another Name

Following the river west from **SAUMUR**, on the D751, you will find the sparkling *rosé d'Anjou*. Or, from **MONTREUIL**, cut overland on the D761 to **BRISSAC-QUINCE**...just 33 kms over a gentle plain.

From the D751, turn left to **BRISSAC-QUINCÉ**, and the fruity wines of the Coteaux de l'Aubance (AOC) with another knock-out, 16th c. chateau. The Anjou is most famous for sweet white and rosé. They were Josephine Bonaparte's favorites. Gamay, Groslot and Pineau d'Aunis are the grapes grown here for the rosé, the Cabernet for the rosé de Cabernet and the Cabernet d'Anjou. Many bear the AOC designation.

From Brissac-Quincé, head south towards **FAYE D'ANJOU** and the sweet wines of the Coteaux du Layon Villages (AOC). In some years, the "noble rot" *Botrytis*, gives a wonderful honey "nose" and flavor, not unlike the Sauternes (Tour 6) of Bordeaux.

After Faye d'Anjou turn left towards (**CHAVAGNES**) and, in two kms., follow the signs towards **THOUARCE**, then take the D125 right to **RABLAY-SUR-LAYON**. There are wineries to visit all along the way.

Three-quarters of the wines of the Loire Valley are white, but in the Anjou, nearly half of the wine produced is rosé. Later, you can compare these with the rosés of Provence, which use different grapes and enjoy a Mediterranean climate, and of Tavel in the Rhone River valley.

Continue on D125 to **ST. LAMBERT-DU-LATTAY** and then towards **LE BREUIL**, crossing the Layon river on D209, skimming the Quarts de Chaume (AOC), and the Bonnezeaux (AOC), more intense versions of the Coteaux du Layon.

Follow the signs towards **ROCHEFORT-SUR-LOIRE** and from there, **SAVENNIERES**, to get across the Loire. Here, a choice awaits: the road left to **ST. GEORGES-SUR-LOIRE**, the Chateau de Serrant, and a bit of the Coteaux de Loire (AOC); or a right turn towards **BOUCHEMAINE**, through the white wine district of the Savennieres (AOC).

Chateau Serrant

Chateau Brissac

After Bouchemaine, keep a sharp eye out for the footbridge over the Maine River at **PRUNIERS** to get into **ANGERS** and its Renaissance houses. In the 6th century, the poet Apollinaire said that Angers was the city filled with the gifts of Bacchus, the God of Wine. They've been making wine in this area for a long time.

If you chose the Chateau de Serrant route, the D23 goes straight back to Angers. Further west, at Nantes, are the sweet Muscadet (AOC) wines, but by now you've had a good taste of the gentle Loire Valley whites and rosés. The Touraine reds are just an introduction. Now, pucker-up, it's time for Bordeaux!

Details & Contacts 3

TERRAIN: Flat, except some elevations along the Layon river. Prevailing winds from the west. IGN #25, Distance: 55 kms.

AOC: ANJOU, COTEAUX DE L'AUBANCE, COTEAUX DU LAYON, COTEAUX DU LAYON VILLAGES, QUARTS DE CHAUME, BONNEZEAUX, SAVENNIERES.

GRAPES: Chenin blanc, Cabernet, Gamay noir a jus blanc, Cabernet franc, Chardonnay, Sauvignon.

FOOD & LODGING: Grand Hotel, 30, rue Rene-Gasnier, Rochefort-sur-Loire. 41.78.70.06.

CHAMBRES D'HOTE: M. Alfred Bidet, 66 Grande Rue, RABLAY-SUR-LAYON, 49190 Rochefort-sur-Loire. 41.78.32.68.
Marthe Blanvillain, Le Patureau, 49190 Rochefort-sur-Loire. 41.78.73.26.

CAMPING: Parc de la Haye. 41.87.36.69. (4.5 km NW of Angers). Open all year.
CM de Varennes, Murs Erigné, Les Ponts de Cé. 41.91.18.59. On N160. (Oct. 15-April)

AJ: Centre d'Accueil du Lac du Maine, Route de Pruniers, 49000 Angers. 41.48.57.01. (9/15-6/15).

WINERY CONTACTS: Domaine de La Roche Moreau, M. Andre Davy, ST. AUBIN DE LUIGNE, 49190 Rochefort-sur-Loire. 41.78.33.18.
Petiteau, BP, 32 rue du Pont Barre, ST. LAMBERT-DU-LATTAY, 49190 Rochefort-sur-Loire. 41.41.70.28.
Chateau de Fesles, M. Boivin, 49380 THOUARCE. 41.91.40.40.
Le Gros Chene, M. Robin-Picherit, FAYE D'ANJOU, 49380 Thouarce. 41.91.41.36.
Domaine des Maurieres, M. Fernand Moron, 8, rue de Perinelle, 49190 Saint-Lambert-du-Lattay. 41.78.30.21.
Chateau de Plaisance, M. H. Rochais, 49190 Rochefort-sur-Loire. 41.78.33.01.
C.I.V.A.S., M. Duchene, 21 Blvd. Foch, 49100 Angers. 41.87.62.57.
Maison du Vin, 5 bis Place Kennedy, 49000 Angers. 41.88.81.13.

BICYCLE REPAIRS: G. Pineau, 36 bis, Boulevard Ayrault, 48000 Angers. 41.88.30.47.

CHATEAUX HOURS: BRISSAC: park & tours, 9:30-11:30, 14:45-17:45. (Oct. 15-Mar. 15, Tuesdays)
SERRANT: July-Aug, 9-6, (Nov.-Palm Sunday; Tuesdays except July/Aug)

Chaume

Domaine de la Roche Moreau

APPELLATION COTEAUX DU LAYON CHAUME CONTRÔLÉE

Mis en bouteille au Domaine par A. DAVY Propriétaire Viticulteur
49190 ST AUBIN DE LUIGNÉ (M L) FRANCE

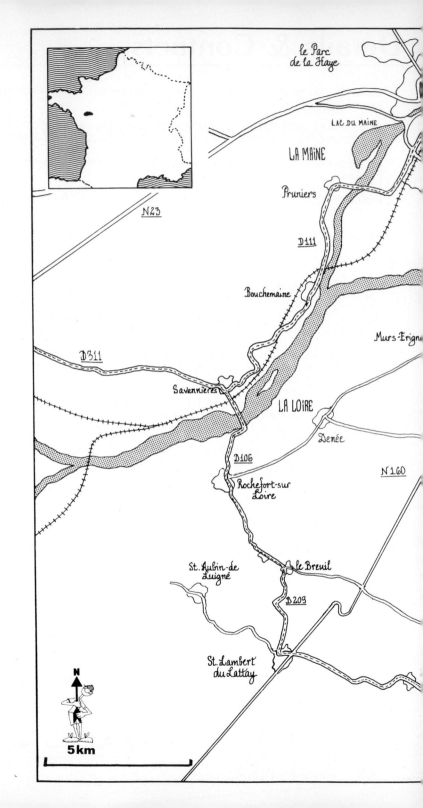

Le Parc de la Haye

LAC DU MAINE

LA MAINE

Pruniers

N23

D111

Bouchemaine

Murs-Érign

D311

Savennières

LA LOIRE

Denée

D106

N160

Rochefort-sur-Loire

St. Aubin-de-Luigné

le Breuil

D209

St. Lambert du Lattay

N

5km

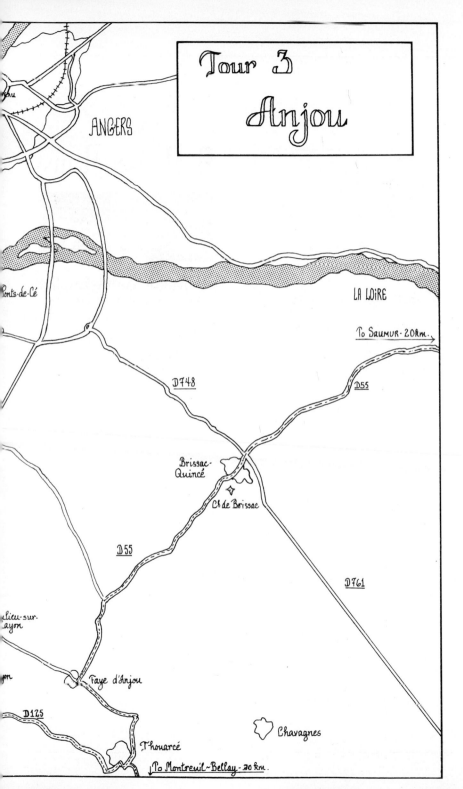

Tour 3
Anjou

ANGERS

Ponts-de-Cé

LA LOIRE

To Saumur - 20km.

D748

D55

Brissac-
Quincé

Ct de Brissac

D55

D761

...lieu-sur-
...ayon

...on Faye d'Anjou

D125

Chavagnes

Thouarcé

To Montreuil-Bellay - 30km.

Château

De Maison Neuve

Montagne Saint-Emilion
APPELLATION MONTAGNE SAINT-ÉMILION CONTRÔLÉE

1982

Michel COUDROY
PROPRIÉTAIRE A MAISON NEUVE
MONTAGNE (GIRONDE) FRANCE
Tel (57) 84 02 23

MIS EN BOUTEILLES AU CHATEAU

75cl

BORDEAUX SUPÉRIEUR
Appellation Bordeaux Supérieur Contrôlée

DISTRIBUÉ PAR
S.C.E. DU CHATEAU GROS BONNET
VITICULTEUR-RÉCOLTANT A FRONSAC - 33126
G.F.A. BOURRET Henry, propriétaire
PRODUIT DE FRANCE

Je
 MR.

Selected Trains Paris — Bordeaux (subject to change)

From Paris (Austerlitz)	09:09	12:00	14:21	17:32	17:45	23:56*
To St. Pierre/d/Corps (Tours)	11:01	14:13		19:28		02:31
To Libourne	13:37	17:24		22:19	.	05:49
To Bordeaux (St. Jean)	13:58	17:46	18:24	22:42	22:16	06:12

*Sleeping car available

From Bordeaux (St. Jean)	09:27	11:46	12:57	14:15	16:55	22:26*
To Libourne	09:48		13:20	14:37	17:17	22:50
To St. Pierre/d/Corps (Tours)	12:06	14:17	16:34	17:15	19:47	
To Paris (Austerlitz)	13:46	16:00	18:43	19:15	21:38	06:10

*Sleeping car available

St. Emilion   Tour

A Pucker in the Mouth

4

The last stop on the train before the city of Bordeaux, **LIBOURNE** retains a friendly charm of 1000 years of wine commerce on the north bank of the Dordogne. The old plaza has a helpful *Office de Tourisme*, and the great St. Emilion region is close by.

Go behind the Libourne *Gare*, east towards SAINT EMILION. Signs will point to the D17E, but look for the smaller road, parallel to D17E and just south of it, which offers a nearly traffic-less ride through Merlot, Cabernet and Cabernet franc (called *Bouchet* regionally)...grapes of the Cotes de Castillon (AOC).

The St. Emilion (AOC) has further limiting classifications: 2 *Premiere Grand Cru Classé*, 9 *Grand Cru Classé*, and 63 *Grand Cru*. The earliest system of classifying French wines was begun by Napoleon III in the Medoc. These wines were first classified in 1954 and are revised every few years. Try to enjoy the wines and don't worry too much about the labeling details.

Merlot, the major grape, grows on both the sandy-gravelly soils and the clay-chalk soils of the region. Note the changes along the route: the best vines will be low to the ground with a rather pitiful canopy of leaves and a few struggling bunches of grapes. They aren't sick, they are just suffering. In the world of wine, the grapes that suffer most produce the best wines (in general). Fortunately, human beings are not brought up on a similar philosophy.

Just before the rise to **ST. EMILION** is Chateau L'Angelus, (Grand Cru Classé). Please note, you'll need to write in advance to visit most of this area's winemakers. Things are more formal here than in the Loire.

The ancient bank of the Dordogne provides a short climb up to the well-preserved village of St. Emilion. Wine shops, boutiques, even a bicycle shop are here.

England, after 1152, controlled the Bordeaux wine region as part of Aquitaine, for several centuries, and the British became fans of the local "Claret," as the British still call red Bordeaux. Actually, "clairet" was and is the local rosé wine, but the name became synonymous with reds for the English.

The Tourist Information Office in St. Emilion is directly across from King Louis VIII's belltower, in the deanery cloisters. Underneath the cobbled streets which wind down the bluff are enormous underground *caves*, old quarries like the caves of the Loire, which serve as ideal wine-storage facilities. At the southern foot of town is Chateau Ausone, in honor of the Roman poet Ausonius, who lived nearby.

Head north from St. Emilion through **CADET** towards **MONTAGNE** and the satellite regions of St. Emilion. The grape remains predominantly Merlot with some Cabernet. At **VACHON**, there is a campground and lake. Up on the hill beyond, is Chateau Cap d'Or.

Turn left at **MONTAGNE** towards POMEROL (AOC), the home of Chateau Petrus. The town is quite unassuming. One hand-painted and slightly weary sign, just beyond the church, advertises a *vente directe*. But those one-branched little grapevines struggling around you bear some of the world's most valuable fruit. It is said the Druids used these wines as part of their religious ceremonies.

Continue west, crossing the N89, a set of railroad tracks and the D910 at LES BILLAUX. The appellations change now; Lelande de Pomerol (AOC) and Neac (AOC). Take the left fork onto the D18E towards GIRARD, then GALGON, turning left on D138 to VILLEGOUGE and the Fronsac (AOC).

A favorite wine region of Charlemagne, who advocated shipment in barrels and storage in wood, Fronsac has the natural military advantage of the bluff. Gauls, Romans, Normans, including Caesar and Charlemagne built fortifications here, and razed those of their enemies. Wines of many villages on the bluff are under the Canon-Fronsac (AOC).

Spectacular views and easy bicycling on this bluff, try to stay up on top, heading towards **MEYNEY** and then **ST. AIGNAN**, where you will have to descend, at last, at **ST. MICHEL DE FRONSAC** and the rather busy D670, a two-lane road with little shoulder. Follow that upriver to **FRONSAC**, a small old town with plenty of wine history, and a short hop to the bridge over the L'Isle river into **LIBOURNE**.

Your next choice is: (A) the train to Bordeaux and the Medoc region (Tour 5) or, (B) a longish ride south and east towards Langon, across the Entre-Deux-Mers (AOC) region to the Sauternes (Tour 6).

Fronsac ◱ *St-Emilion* ▦ *Pomerol* ☐

Lalande de Pomerol ▤ *Montagne St-Emilion* ▧

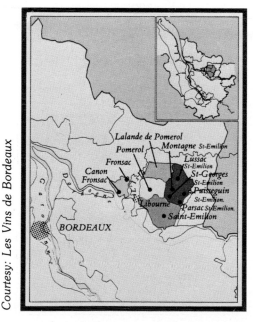

Courtesy: Les Vins de Bordeaux

Don't be blinded by the Crus.

41

4 Details & Contacts

TERRAIN: The bluff above the river bank affords a climb, but on the plateau above or along the river, all is fairly flat. IGN #46. Distance: 47 km.

AOC: BORDEAUX, ST. EMILION, (and various combinations of the name), COTES DE CASTILLON, POMEROL, FRONSAC, CANON-FRONSAC, LALANDE-DE-POMEROL.

GRAPES: Merlot, Cabernet Sauvignon, Cabernet Franc (Bouchet), Malbec.

FOOD & LODGING: Hotel Loubat, 32 rue Chanzy (near *gare*), 33500 Libourne. 57.51.17.58.
Le Landais Restaurant, behind Hotel Loubat. 33500 Libourne. 57.74.07.40.
Le Gril Restaurant, Libourne plaza.
Hostellerie de Plaisance, Place du Clocher, 33330 Saint Emilion. 57.24.72.32. Open all year. †
Syndicat d'Initiative, "Le Doyenne", Place des Creneaux, 33330 St. Emilion. 57.24.72.03.
Syndicat Viticole de St. Emilion, BP 15, 33330 St. Emilion. 57.24.72.17.

CAMPING: CM La Barbane, 33330 St. Emilion. 57.24.75.80. (Nov.-Feb.)

WINERY CONTACTS: Chateau L'Angelus, M. De Bouard, 33330 St. Emilion. 57.24.71.39. Open every day.
Chateau Ausone, 33330 St. Emilion. 57.24.70.94. †
Chateau Cap d'Or, ST. GEORGES, St. Emilion. A wide range of labels here. Open daily.
Chateau Soutard, M. Francois de Ligneres. 33330 St. Emilion. 57.24.70.93. †
Chateau Maison-Neuve, M. Coudroy, Montagne-St. Emilion. 57.84.02.23.
Chateau Petrus, 33500 Pomerol. 57.51.78.97. †
Chateau Mazeris-Bellevue, M. Jacques Bussier, 33145 Saint-Michel-de-Fronsac. 56.24.98.19. Open daily.
Chateau Gros. Bonnet, M. Henri Bourret, 33126 Fronsac. Open daily.
J. Janoueix, 37 rue Pline-Parmentier, 33500 Libourne. 56.51.41.86.

BICYCLE REPAIRS: At Libourne, St. Emilion, Fronsac.

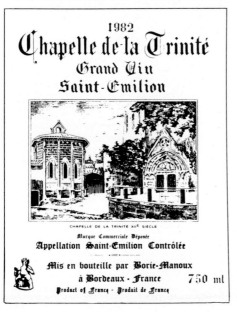

A little wine in the water bottle shortens the kilometers.

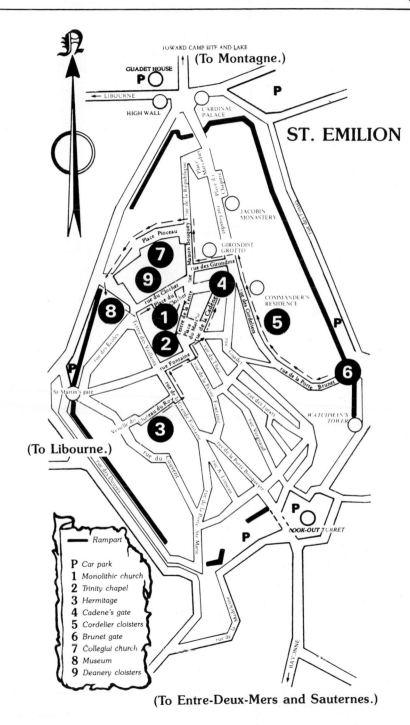

ST. EMILION

(To Montagne.)

(To Libourne.)

Rampart

P Car park
1 Monolithic church
2 Trinity chapel
3 Hermitage
4 Cadene's gate
5 Cordelier cloisters
6 Brunet gate
7 Collegial church
8 Museum
9 Deanery cloisters

(To Entre-Deux-Mers and Sauternes.)

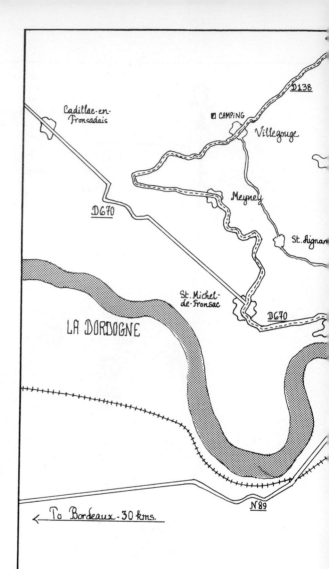

Cadillac-en-
Fronsadais

☑ CAMPING

Villegouge

D138

Meyney

St. Aignan

D670

St. Michel-
de-Fronsac

LA DORDOGNE

D670

To Bordeaux - 30 kms.

N89

Tour 4
St. Emilion

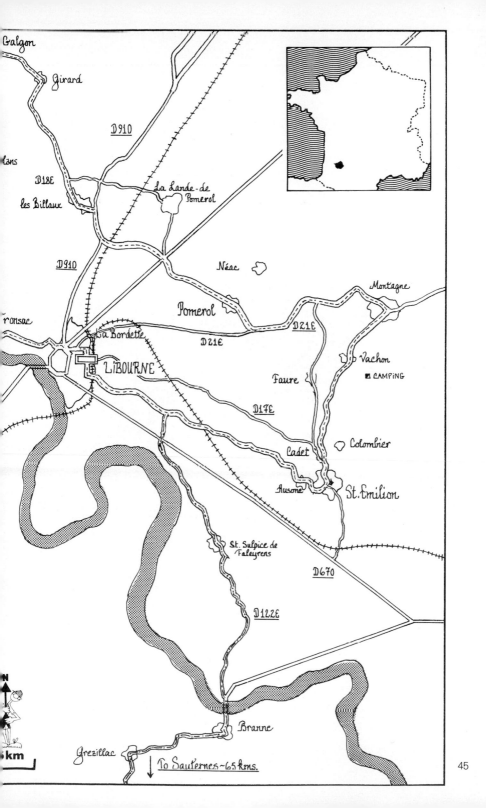

Galgon

Girard

D910

Mans

D18E

les Billaux

La Lande-de-Pomerol

D910

Néac

Montagne

Pomerol

D21E

Fronsac

La Bordette

D21E

LIBOURNE

Faure

Vachon

CAMPING

D17E

Colombier

Cadet

Ausone

St. Emilion

St. Sulpice de Faleyrens

D670

D122E

N

km

Branne

Grezillac

To Sauternes ~ 65 kms.

5

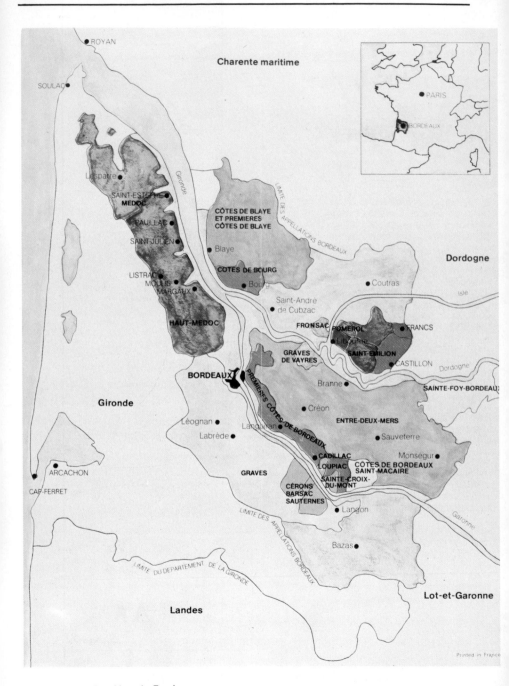

Courtesy: Les Vins de Bordeaux.

Medoc   Tour

Downriver to "High" Medoc 5

The city of Bordeaux is great for bicyclists who like downtown Pittsburg and east Los Angeles. It is the wine marketing capital of the region and has been for centuries, but is skirted by urban sprawl. The helpful Maison du Vin is downtown. Several wine shippers here offer tours of their blending and bottling facilities, if called in advance. The road north towards Pauillac leads to the Medoc (AOC), the road south towards Langon and the Sauternes (AOC) (Tour 6).

The Medoc (AOC) begins only a half-hour out of town. Follow the river north and watch for the signs to **MACAU**. The main route, D2, winds through calm, flat country, crossing the little stream, Jalle de Blanquefort, the official beginning of the Haut Medoc (AOC). Just north of Macau's few stone buildings in Labarde are Chateau Dauzac (Grand Cru) and Chateau Siran, among others.

In 1855 under orders from Napoleon III, each Medoc vineyard holding was formally classified. There are now 4 "first growths" (Ch. Margaux, Ch. Latour, Ch. Mouton Rothschild, Ch. Lafite), 14 "second growths", 14 thirds, 11 fourths and 18 fifths. But a lot can go wrong with a winery operation in all those years, and plenty of good winemakers whose greatgreatgrandfathers didn't happen to be making great wine at the time, should not be overlooked in this region.

The Medoc is actually the youngest winegrowing area of Bordeaux, just a few centuries old. It is a credit to the development of sophisticated viticultural practices that tease great wines from the pebbly soil and the varying limestone and clay base. The forests to the west protect the region from cold Atlantic winds, and the Gulf Stream helps explain the special micro-climate. The growers have chosen Cabernet and Merlot, wisely, making only red wines.

In addition to the growths or *crus*, there are 8 appellations within the Medoc: Medoc, Haut Medoc, then the 6 villages of Margaux, Moulis, Listrac, Saint-Julien, Pauillac, and Saint Estephe. The soil varies, but the vines are tough, sending their roots 15 feet down into the subsoil, withstanding long, dry summers and cool winters...and making legendary, long-aging wines in the "good" years.

5

At **MACAU**, the more direct route from Bordeaux, the D2E, joins the D2, continuing, more heavily traveled, towards **MARGAUX**. Honorary public relations director of the Medoc must be Alexis Lichine, a Russian-born immigrant to France, educated in the USA. He bought the Chateau Prieuré in 1951, just after the war had left many of France's greatest chateaux in ruin. With money from the sale of his wine distribution company, Lichine has restored the Chateau Prieuré Lichine to its former glory.

He offers a friendly tour of his *chais*, as the wine cellars of Medoc are called. Everyone speaks English and sometimes family members are the guides. To get a glimpse of the well-furnished chateau, ask to sign the guest book.

At **MARGAUX**, the Dordogne and the Garonne join, forming the wide Gironde, muddy and slow. From the 11th century, after harvest and in the spring, thousands of ships from England and Holland choked this river, waiting to load the "tonneaux" barrels at Bordeaux. To this day, ships' cargo is measured in wine "tonneaux", 900 litres.

The rich and powerful merchants of Bordeaux forbade loading of wine downriver from their city. That is one reason why the Medoc was late to develop: the wine had to be hauled upriver, overland, to Bordeaux for shipment.

PAUILLAC is the peaceful heart of the Haut Medoc, further downriver the Medoc (AOC) wines are less intense. There is a modern Maison du Vin on the waterfront and a bicycle shop next to the church in the center of town.

Just north of Pauillac, across the road from Chateau Mouton and Chateau Lafite, Shell Oil has a large oil refinery. Across the river, a huge electricity plant looms. Not the most traditional setting, but among these hills, new clones of Cabernet and Merlot are improving vineyard production, stainless steel and air-conditioned transport are increasing quality production and distribution. One takes the good with the bad.

At **ST. ESTEPHE**, near the end of the Haut Medoc, there is a Maison du Vin, as well as several small *vente directe*. Note how the soil changes, now, from those gravelly soils and tortured vines of the Haut Medoc's viticultural sadism.

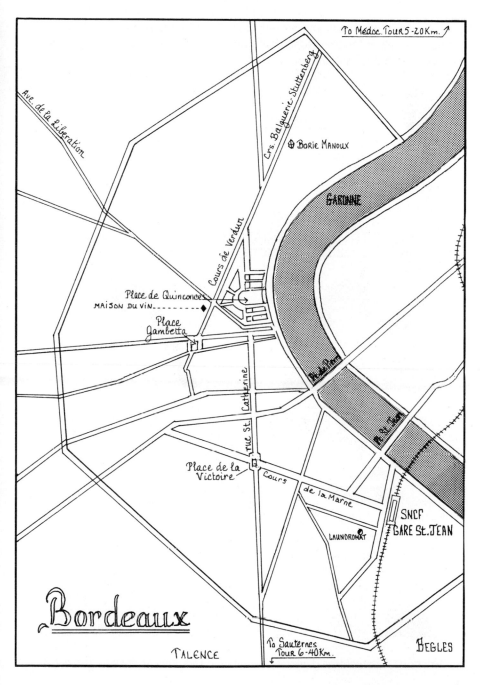

West towards **VERTHEUIL**, the soil gets darker, the vines a bit taller and bushier. Cross the D2E and continue to **CISSAC-MEDOC** with the scent of pine trees and a sandy soil. The Chateaux are close by, and the museum at Mouton-Rothschild open except in August. The D4E goes back to **PAUILLAC** and the weekday commuter train to Bordeaux.

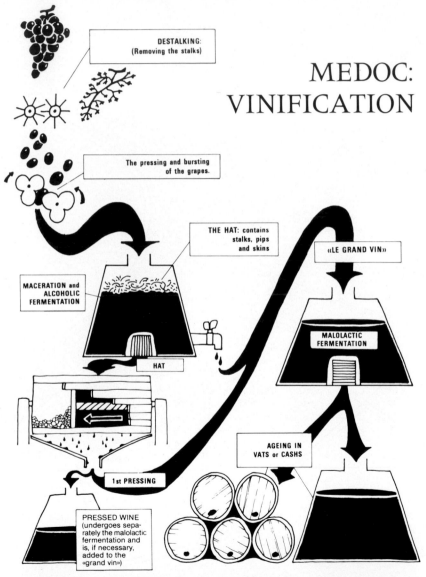

MEDOC: VINIFICATION

DESTALKING: (Removing the stalks)

The pressing and bursting of the grapes.

THE HAT: contains stalks, pips and skins

«LE GRAND VIN»

MACERATION and ALCOHOLIC FERMENTATION

MALOLACTIC FERMENTATION

HAT

AGEING IN VATS or CASHS

1st PRESSING

PRESSED WINE (undergoes separately the malolactic fermentation and is, if necessary, added to the «grand vin»)

Courtesy: Groupement D'Interet Economique Des Vins du Medoc, Bordeaux.

Details & Contacts 5

TERRAIN: Following the gentle "left" bank of the river, occasional winds off the ocean. IGN Map #46. Distance: 40 km.

AOC: HAUT MEDOC, MEDOC, MARGAUX, LISTRAC, MOULIS, SAINT-JULIEN, PAUILLAC, and SAINT-ESTEPHE.

GRAPES: predominantly Cabernet Sauvignon, with Cabernet franc, Merlot, Carmenere, Malbec, Petit-Verdot.

FOOD & LODGING: Hotel d'Amboise, 22 Rue de la Vielle Tour, (near Hotel de Ville) 33000 Bordeaux. 56.81.62.67.
Le Relais de Medoc, LAMARQUE, 33460 Margaux. 56.58.92.27. †
Le Relais de Manoir, Route de la Shell, 33250 PAUILLAC. 56.59.05.47. †
Hotel France-Angleterre, quai A de Pichon, 33250 PAUILLAC. 56.59.01.20.
Restaurant Le Plaisonier, M. & Mme. W. Vierne, (next door to Hotel F-A) PAUILLAC. 56.59.23.55.

CHAMBRES D'HOTE: Mme. Meyre, Chateau Cap Leon Verin, DONISSAN, 33480 Listrac. 56.58.20.44.
Mme R. Roux, Chateau Biston, MOULIS, 33480 Castelnau. 56.58.22.13.
Mme. M. Tardat, Cantemerle, VERTHEUIL, 33250 Pauillac. 56.41.96.24.
No camping, but campsites at the beach, just west of the Medoc.

AJ: 22 cours Barbey, 33800 BORDEAUX. 56.91.59.51. (Jan.)

WINERY CONTACTS: Conseil Interprofessionel du Vin de Bordeaux (CIVB), 1 Cours du XXX Juillet, 33000 Bordeaux. 56.52.82.82. (They will organize 1-5 day tours of the wineries on request.)
Borie-Manoux, M. Philippe E. Casteja, 86, Cours Balguerie-Stuttenberg, 33300 Bordeaux. 56.48.57.57. (weekends). By appointment, tours available of their extensive bottling and shipping operation.
Chateau Rausan-Segla, Eschenauer, 42 ave E. Counord, 33077 Bordeaux. 56.81.58.90.
Chateau Siran, M. Miailhe, BP 35, 33024 Bordeaux cedex. 56.81.35.01.
Chateau Prieure-Lichine (Grand Cru), M. Alexis Lichine, CANTENAC, 33460 Margaux. 56.88.36.28. Open 9-19, every day. English spoken.
Chateau Tour du Haut-Moulin (Grand Cru), M.L. Poitou, Cussac le Vieux, CUSSAC-FORT-MEDOC, 33460 Margaux. 56.58.91.10. Open daily (12-15).
Chateau Clarke, CASTELEU-EN-MEDOC, 33480 Listrac. 56.88.88.00. †
Chateau Beychevelle (Cru Classe), M. Achille-Fould, ST. JULIEN-BEYCHEVELLE, 33250 Pauillac. 56.59.23.00. Open 9:30-17:45, M-F.
Chateau Batailley (Grand Cru Classe), 33250 Pauillac. 56.59.01.13. (Sunday).
Chateau Mouton Rothschild (Ire Cru), M. Raoul Blondin, LE POUYALET, 33250 Pauillac. (56) 59.22.22. Open in July by appointment. (August). Museum. English spoken.
Chateau Cos D'Estournel (Cru Classe), M. Jean Coudoin, ST. ESTEPHE, 33250 Pauillac. 56.44.11.37. Open July & August, 12:30-18:30 (Monday). English spoken.

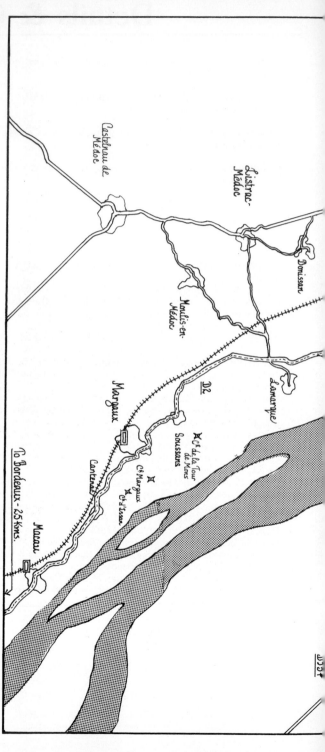

To Bordeaux - 25 Kms.

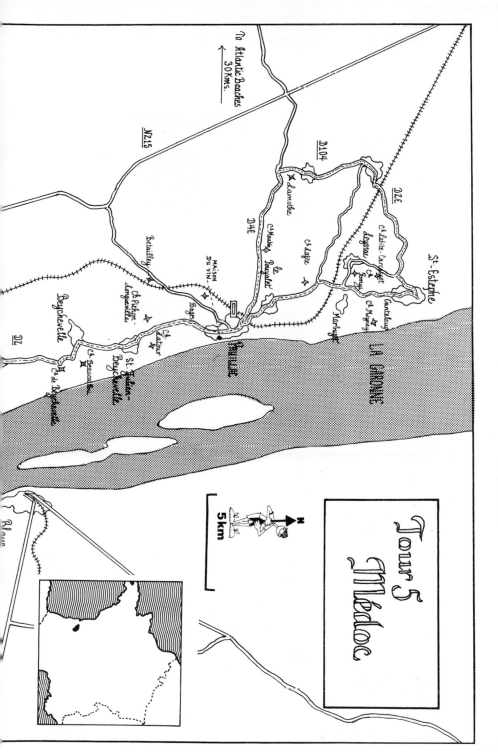

To Atlantic Beaches
30 Kms.

N215

D104

D2E

La Mothe

Cⁱ Moulin

Cⁱ Lafite

Cⁱ Calon-Ségur Lagrasse

St-Estèphe

Cⁱ de Marquis

Cantacrolle

Marquet

LA GIRONNE

D4E

Cⁱ Mouton

le
Pouyalet

MAISON
DU VIN

Bages

Retaillan

Cⁱ Pichon-
Longueville

PAUILLAC

Cⁱ
Latour

St-Julien-
Beycheville

Cⁱ Gruaud-Larose

D2

Beycheville

Cⁱ de Beycheville

N

5km

Tour 5
Médoc

Blaye

Grand Cru Classé en 1855
Monument Historique

33210 Preignac
Tèl:(56) 63.28.67

Four-wire "plate" pruning in Sauternes.

Sauternes

Serious Sweets

FROM BORDEAUX, the wine country of Graves (AOC) begins just 10 kms. south. The difficulty is getting out of town: Leave the **GARE ST. JEAN** and follow the Cours de la Marne, heading straight north (although you are ultimately heading south) towards the **PLACE DE LA VICTOIRE**. There is a laundromat, *Lavagomatic*, 200 meters from the gare on the left.

Take the Cours de la Somme at the Place de la Victoire, a hard left, east towards **BARRIERE DE TOULOUSE** and keep straight. You are now on the N113 towards the Graves, the dry white wine region of Bordeaux which follows the Gironde south to the Sauternes (AOC).

Smaller routes through the vineyards begin at Chateau de la Prade. Follow the signs to **ST. SELVE**, **ST. MICHEL** and **ILLATS**, and cross the autoroute towards **PREIGNAC**. Which road? It's not critical, just wander south and east and look for signs to Chateau Caillou and Chateau Piada, or stop where you please.

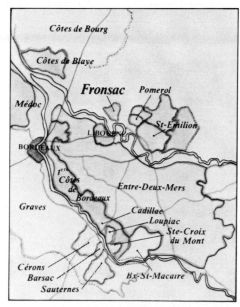

Courtesy: Les Vins de Bordeaux.

"Gardez la ligne" does not mean "watch the road." It means "watch your figure" . . .

If you prefer a more direct route, take the N113 all the way. It is a little boring and the road offers no shoulder for cyclists and few wine stops before **BARSAC**.

FROM LIBOURNE, take the D122 across the Dordogne towards **BRANNE** and ride south and east through the wooded white country of Entre-Deux-Mers (AOC). At **GREZILLAC**, watch for **TARGON** and the D11, a left turn that will take you all the way to **CADILLAC**, through the vineyards "between the two seas." Actually, the region is between two rivers, the Dordogne and the Garonne. The name dates from the 16th century, and today 2.5 million gallons of wine are produced under this appellation. The red wines from this area rate Bordeaux and Bordeaux Superior (AOC) labels. The spacing between vines is greater here, and the growth more vigorous, than in St. Emilion. Semillon, Sauvignon blanc, Muscadet and Ugni blanc grapes make the white wine.

At **CADILLAC** the Premieres Cotes de Bordeaux (AOC) feature sweet white wines and a preview of the great sweet Sauternes across the river.

Cross the Garonne at **CADILLAC**, into **CERONS**, and take the N113 south (left) towards **BARSAC** (AOC), or plunge into the lovely back country lanes towards the Barsac vineyards.

FROM LANGON, follow the road south towards (**BAZAS**), but cut off to the smaller roads at **LA MOURASSE**, following the signs to **MAZERES**, then towards **ROAILLAN** and the ancient castle of Roquetaillade. (See if the Loire Valley has saturated your enthusiasm for chateaux.)

Selected Trains Bordeaux — Les Arcs

From Bordeaux	06:41	11:25	14:38	22:37*
To Marseille — (TGV)	13:03	18:43	21:00	15:57
From Marseille — (TGV)	13:17	19:23	22:02	06:15
To Les Arcs		20:48		
To St Raphael	14:49	21:08	23:32	07:56
*Sleeping car available				

Château de Malle

This unique region, from Barsac to Sauternes (AOC) grows Semillon, Sauvignon blanc and some Muscadel grapes for a remarkable, long aging, sweet white wine, honeyed with the "noble rot", botrytis. The vineyards are trained in careful rows, held like plates by four wires, and the harvest is a series of passes between the vines, hand-picking each grape as it ripens and rots.

After the castle, head towards **SAUTERNES** and sample at the Maison du Sauternes on the little town square. The Auberge restaurant there has excellent food.

There is a chateau-hotel, Chateau Commarque, just south of Sauternes, run by a former bicycle racer, Jeffrey Kenyon-May. It has a pool and a restaurant.

With bicycles, you can't say you ran out of gas.

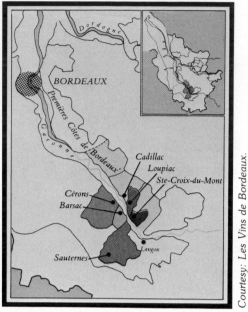

Courtesy: Les Vins de Bordeaux.

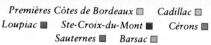

Premières Côtes de Bordeaux □   *Cadillac* □
Loupiac ▧   *Ste-Croix-du-Mont* ▨   *Cérons* ▨
Sauternes ▩   *Barsac* ▨

Bring your bicycle on the train . . . . where else would you find such a pleasant traveling companion?

Call ahead to visit Chateau Lamothe, Clos Haut Peyraguey, and Chateau de la Tour Blanche, all nearby, on the north side of Sauternes. You can ride around the famous Chateau d'Yquem, but there are no tastings or tours...the honey-aged wines of this area can sell for over $100/bottle, and great vintages are rarely for sale, much less for tasting.

Continue through the pleasant maze of vineyards and pine woods north to Chateau Malle, and from there to **PREIGNAC** and **BARSAC** vineyards.

Catch the train at Langon east to Marseilles, or go back to Bordeaux from any of the small gares.

TERRAIN: Rolling across Entre Deux Mers. One hill at Sauternes. Otherwise, flat. IGN #56. Distances: Libourne to Cadillac 55 km.; tour: 40 km; Langon to Bordeaux, 50 km.

AOC: BORDEAUX, BORDEAUX SUPERIOR, ENTRE-DEUX-MERS, COTES DE BORDEAUX, GRAVES (dry white), GRAVES SUPERIEURES (sweet white), CERONS, BARSAC, SAUTERNES.

GRAPES: Semillion, Sauvignon blanc, Muscadel (whites).

FOOD & LODGING: Hotel Commerce, 33410 Cadillac
Claude Derroze Hotel, 33210 Langon.
Chateau de Commarque, Jeffrcy Kenyon-May, 33210 Sauternes. 56.63.65.94.
Chateau de Rolland, 33720 Barsac. 56.27.15.75. on RN113. [†]
La Grappe d'Or restaurant, Cerons.

CHAMBRES D'HOTE: M.J. Fauques, Les Berdigots, 33730 VILLANDRAUT. 56.25.30.79
M.J. Guillot de Suduirot, Chateau de Broustaret, RIONS, 33410 Cadillac. 56.62.96.97
M. Jose Chauchard, La Grande Metairie, 33230 COUTRAS. 57.49.13.00.

CAMPING: CM Allees Marine, 2 Ave. de l'Hippodrome, Langon. (Oct.-May).

WINERY CONTACTS: Syndicat Viticole, M. Louis Richard, Place de l'eglise, Barsac, 33720 Podensac. 56.27.15.44.
Syndicat Viticole de l'A.O.C. Sauternes, M.J. Frouin, 33118 Sauternes. 56.63.60.37.
Chateau Lamothe, M. Guignard, 33210 Sauternes. 56.63.60.28.
Ch. La Tour Blanche (Premiere Cru), Bommes. 56.63.61.55.
Clos Haut Peyraguey, M. Pauly, Bommes. 56.63.61.53.
Chateau de Malle, M. le Comte de Bournazel, 33210 Preignac. 56.63.28.67.
Chateau Piada, M. Jean Lalande, Barsac, 33720 Podensac. 56.27.16.13.

BICYCLE REPAIRS: Cycles Peugeot, 8 Cours des Fosses, 33210 Langon. 56.63.17.52. Or in Cadillac.

CHATEAU HOURS: Ch. Roquetaillade, 10-12, 14-19. (Nov. 15-Mar. 1). 33210 Langon. 56.63.24.16.

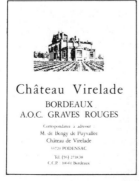

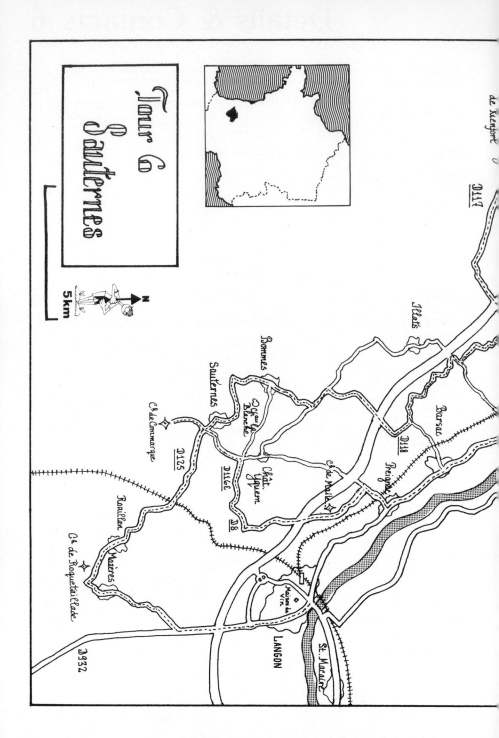

Tour de Sauternes

5km N

de Rergort

D1110

D1110

Illats

Barsac

D118

Bommes

Château Blanche

Sauternes

Château Yquem

Château de Commarque

D125

D116E

D8

Château de Malle

Preignac

Barillon Mazères

Château de Roquetaillade

Maison du Vin

LANGON

St. Macaire

D932

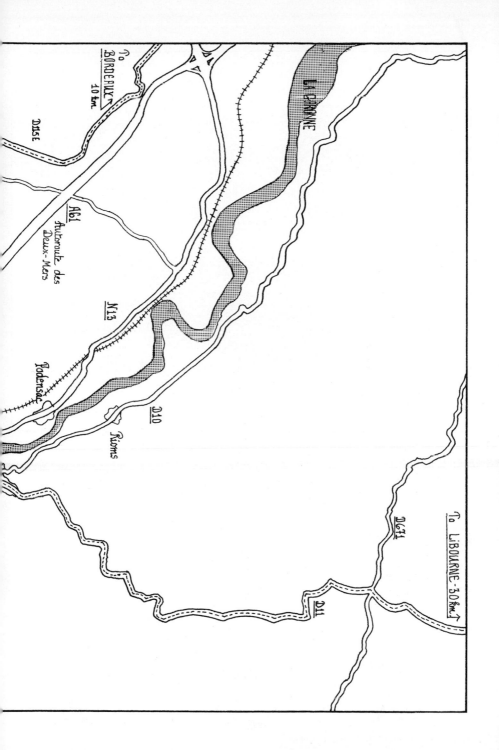

To
BORDEAUX
10 km.

D1SE

A61
Autoroute des
Deux-Mers

N13

Podensac

LA GARONNE

D10

Rioms

D11

D671

To LiBOURNE - 3.0 km.

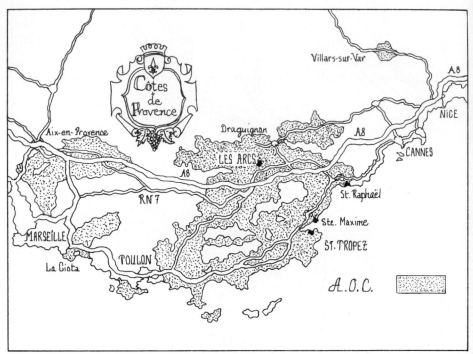

Courtesy: Comité Interprofessionnel des Vins Côtes de Provence

Gobelet traditional pruning.

Provence   Tour

The Backside of St. Tropez 7

FROM BORDEAUX, the train goes east to Avignon, and the Cotes du Rhone (Tour 8), or change here for Marseilles, Toulon and Les Arcs and the Cotes de Provence (AOC), named from the latin, *Provincia Romana*.

FROM PARIS, the TGV bullet train goes as far as Toulon.

Greek amphora found in the sea off Marseilles prove that the Provence has been producing and exporting wine since the 6th century B.C. That early wine was probably a light red variety not unlike the rosé for which this region is famous today. The juice of 11 varieties of red grapes stays on the skins just long enough to impart the proper color, and is then pressed off, cool-fermented, and a fruity product results. One grape of the blend, the Syrah, was brought here by the Persians.

A good rosé is subtle and dry, with a touch of spritz, a fresh fruity nose, and a lovely salmon color. It should be drunk young! The Maures mountain vineyards here also produce some full-bodied reds.

There is excellent cycling, (and mountain climbs for those eager for hard exercise), ancient Roman ruins, Provencal villages of Mediterranean pinks and sands...dark blue skies...grey-green olive trees...fields of lavendar...all within an afternoon's cycling of St. Tropez and the Mediterranean Sea.

Unfortunately, beach communities have indigenous problems: sandy roads choked with summer holiday traffic; over-priced motels and over-booked camp grounds; shopping centers *Geant Casino*, and frantic foot traffic of toasted tourists with too little to do.

But the vineyards provide a peaceful world of dusty pink chateaux and towns as old as the Roman Road which passed through the valley.

Les Arcs is a frequent train-stop between Marseille and Nice. The *Comite Interprofessional des Vins des Cotes de Provence* and the local Maison du Vin are across the main road from the gare. There are maps and explanations of the wines, in English, but no tastings.

Turn right into **LES ARCS**, a lovely old Provencal village, and at the main square, watch for signs to **CHATEAU ST. ROSALINE**. Follow them to this historical chapel and winery. The history of wine in the eastern part of France is closely associated with the Church, which owned the best vineyards during the Middle Ages.

Note the red clay soil of these valley vineyards, and the patchwork of different grape varieties. Continue north towards **LA MOTTE**, taking the small road due north to D59, which goes to **DRAGUIGNAN** and the *Syndicat d'Initiative* on the main street. It's a healthy climb, and there is more to come. (If you don't feel like climbing, return to Les Arcs and continue on towards the coast.)

In summer, the prevailing wind is warm and from the southwest. It can blow with a vengence, but the mountains protect you on the climb from Draguignan to **LORGUES** on the D562. The road mounts sharply then winds through the hills. Note how the soil changes. A sign for Chateau la Selle on the left about 5 km. from Draguignan leads to a fine vineyard, part of Domaine Ott, and a stunning view of Lorgues, below, but the road is gravelly and poor for cycling.

Continuing along the D562, stop at the Cooperative at Lorgues for tasting, then drop down on the D10 to **TARADEAU** and follow the signs back towards (**LES ARCS**), stopping in at Chateau de Saint-Martin, an historic winery with 15th century cellars. It will be flat from here to the coast, now, following the D7 towards **FREJUS**, founded by Caesar in 49 B.C., then a right towards **ROQUEBRUNE** and **ST. AVAULF** by the sea.

Follow the coast south to **ST. TROPEZ**, along the Cote d'Azur. Just before this bikini town is a winery cooperative, Les Maitres Vignerons de St. Tropez, with free tastings and a wide assortment of labels. Chateau Minuty, on the road to **RAMATUELLE**, is 2 kms. away in a peaceful valley full of vineyards.

To get back to the railroad service, go east on N559 to **TOULON**, 70 kms., or return the 20 kms. to **ST. AVAULF** and **ST. RAPHAEL**, an old and dignified resort with the finest beach on this stretch of the Mediterranean. The local train service from here to Cannes and Nice takes *bagage a main*, so your bicycle rides for free. For Tour 9, catch the express trains to Marseilles and Avignon.

How They Make Rosé Wine

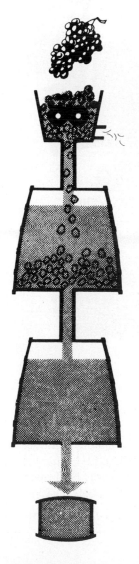

Rosé wine

Red grapes are crushed and put into the cuvee with skins on. When proper color is achieved, usually within 24 hours, the skins are removed, and the juice fermented as with white wine.

Temperature control during fermentation gives a fruitier result.

To St. Raphael (20 km.)

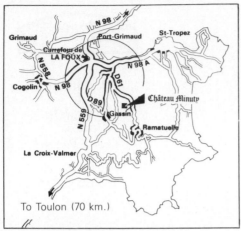

To Toulon (70 km.)

St. Tropez area.

CHATEAU
BARBEYROLLES

COTES DE PROVENCE
Appellation Côtes de Provence Contrôlée

1981

CETTE BOUTEILLE PORTE LE

N° 17531

MIS EN BOUTEILLE AU CHATEAU

RÉGINE SUMEIRE, PROPRIÉTAIRE-RÉCOLTANT
GASSIN, 83990 SAINT-TROPEZ

75cl   PRODUCE OF
FRANCE

This ride is not for marginal riders.

HIGH ALTITUDE ALTERNATE ROUTE: For a more strenuous afternoon, after **LORQUES**, take the road to **TARADEAU** then to **VIDAUBAN** and continue south on D48 over the mountains to St. Tropez. Allow three hours by this route, and stop in the charming mountain village, **LA GARDE FREINET**, at the top, but it is a climb!

Details & Contacts 7

TERRAIN: Steep hill climbs, but flat in the valley and along the coast. Strong prevailing winds, from south in summer, from north in spring. IGN Map #68. Distance: Les Arcs circle: 40 km. Les Arcs to St. Tropez: 60 km.

AOC: COTES DE PROVENCE

GRAPES: (reds & rosés) Carignan, Cinsault, Grenache, Mourvedre, Tobourn, Syrah, Barbaroux, Cabernet Sauvignon, Calitor. (white) Clairette, Semillion, Ugni blanc, Rolle.

FOOD & LODGING: Hostellerie du Parc, 12 rue Jean Jaures, RN7, 83340 Le Luc en Provence. 94.60.70.01. †
Le San Pedro, 83700 St. Rafael-Valescure. 94.52.10.24. † (Oct.15-Easter)

CHAMBRES D'HOTE: Mme. Martine Gurnari, Quartier de Bertaud, 83580 Gassin, 94.56.14.79.
Robert Ladouceur, "Qu. La Rouilliere", 83350 Ramatuelle. 94.56.18.47.
Gustave Giraud, Lei Souco, 83350 Ramatuelle. 94.79.80.22.
Rene DeGuine, STE. MAXIME, 83120 Plan de la Tour. 94.96.06.88.
M. Valentin Molas, Qu. les Vigneaux, 83360 Grimaud. 94.43.23.91.

CAMPING: Camping la Prairie, LE MUY. 94.44.42.22. (Jan.-May).
Le Colombier, FREJUS (NW on D4). 94.95.44.31. (Nov.-Easter).
Camping a la Croix-du-Sud, D93 toward St. Tropez, (RAMATUELLE) Loumede. 94.79.80.84. (Nov.-April).
Parc Montana, NW of GASSIN off N559. 94.56.13.03. (Nov.-Jan).
Beausejour les Tasses, RN98 at ST. RAPHAEL. 94.95.03.67. (Nov.-Mar.15).

AJ: Domaine de Bellevue, rue Grisolle, 83600 FREJUS. 94.52.18.75.
Open all year. 83680 LA GARDE-FREINET. 94.43.60.05. (Oct.-Mar 15).

WINERY CONTACTS: Comité Interprofessionnel des Vins des Cotes de Provence, 3 ave. Jean-Jaures, 83460 Les Arcs. 94.73.33.38.
Chateau St. Roseline, Baron de Rasque de Laval, 83460 Les Arcs. 94.73.32.57. (weekends).
Chateau de Selle, M. Olivier Ott, Rt. D73, 83460 Taradeau. 94.68.86.86. (12-14).
La Lorgaise Cooperative, Route de Draguignan, 83510 Lorgues. 94.73.70.10.
Chateau de St. Martin, Mme. la Contesse Gasquet, 83460 Taradeau. 94.73.02.01. (Sundays).
Les Maitres Vignerons de St. Tropez, GASSIN, 83990 St. Tropez. 94.56.32.04.
Chateau Minuty, M. Matton, GASSIN, 83990 St. Tropez. 94.56.12.09.
Chateau Barbeyrolles, Mme. Regine Sumeire, GASSIN, 83990 St. Tropez. 94.56.33.58.

BICYCLE REPAIRS: In Les Arcs, Draguignan, Lorgues, St. Tropez, St. Maxime, St. Raphael.

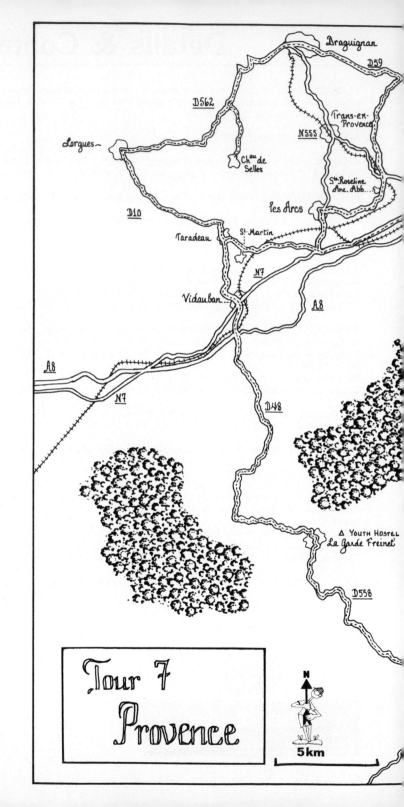

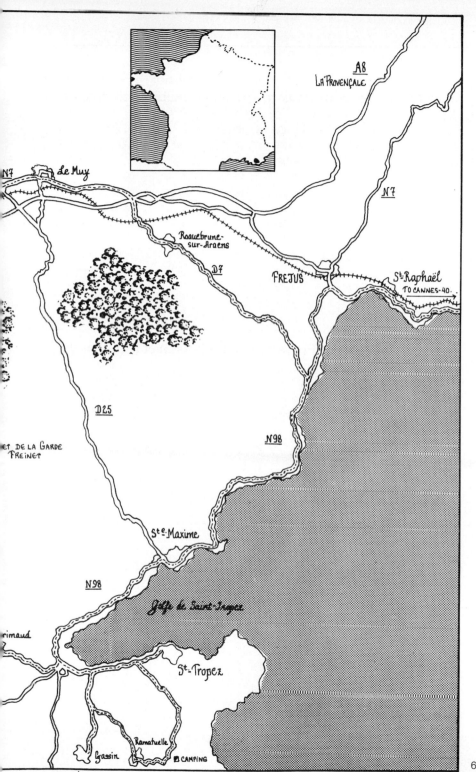

Selected Trains from Paris to Provence (subject to change)

Paris (Gare de Lyon)	09:40	10:23†		20:24*	22:16*
Dijon	12:17			23:52	
Avignon	16:08	14:10			
Marseille	17:11	15:03	(change)	05:06	
Toulon	18:07	15:52	15:55	06:13	06:53
Les Arcs	18:45		16:32	06:53	07:44
St. Raphael	19:07		16:50	07:15	08:04

†TGV *Sleeping car available

Selected Trains from Provence to Paris (subject to change)

St. Raphael	09:51	11:38			14:58		17:29	20:49*	22:13*
Les Arcs	10:14	11:55			15:15		17:46	21:07	
Toulon	10:57	12:32	(change)		15:55		18:25	21:47	23:03
Marseille	11:46	13:38		14:00†	16:34	16:51†	19:26		
Avignon	12:45			14:51		17:42	20:32		
Dijon	16:40								05:14
Paris (Lyon)	19:16			18:40		21:48		06:21	08:14

†TGV *Sleeping car available

"On yer bike!" means "Get lost!" in northern England.

Cotes Du Rhone

Take 13 grapes and big round stones...

Many of the grape varieties of Provence were brought up the Rhone river by the Greeks, and later by the Romans. The Aurelian Way ran all the way from Rome to the Rhone Valley. Eight varieties are specified for the intense reds of the Cotes du Rhone (AOC), but Chateauneuf-du-Pape (AOC) is allowed 13.

AVIGNON is a beautifully preserved medieval fortress town that hosts a summer-long art & drama festival. Something is always happening. There is a *Maison du Vin* upstairs at the Tourist Office on the street running straight into town from the *gare*.

The vineyards begin about 15 kms north of town, just over the bluff on the other side of the river. Take the bridge (*Sur le pont, d'Avignon, on y danse, on y danse...*) towards (**VILLENEUVE**) but follow the signs to **BAGNOLS** on the other side, climbing over the bank and cruising past **LES ANGLES**, north to **BAGNOLS**.

The road to **TAVEL** cuts off to the left and the vineyards begin. The big round stones were a gift from a glacier. It looks like the vines are growing with no soil at all. Tavel has an hospitable *cooperative* with *degustations* and several private establishments, as well. They traditionally make rosé wines exclusively.

Turn back to the river, now, and **ROQUEMAURE**, an ancient shipping capital on the Rhone, little changed in centuries. There is wine here, too, of the appellation, Lirac (AOC). Cross the bridge towards **(ORANGE)**, then turn right, following the river back downstream to **CHATEAUNEUF-DU-PAPE** (AOC).

Chateauneuf-du-Pape was the summer residence of the Popes at Avignon during the 14th century, and is now a town dedicated to wine. If you aren't pooped, a spin around the vineyards would be interesting, about 6 kms, marked *Circuit de Chateauneuf-du-Pape*. You climb up to the round-rocked vineyards to the north and west of the town. These rocks reflect sunshine back up to the hanging grapes, increasing their sugar content, and creating an intense, highly-alcoholic character.

There are almost 3000 hectares (x2.4 = acres) in the AOC area, triple what existed for a millenia before World War II. Then the Caterpillar tractor allowed vineyard workers to conquer more of the stoney terrain.

The town is full of wineries, including Pere Anselme, with a good tour and tasting of their wide selection of Cotes du Rhone wines. This will be your chance to get a broad perspective on the various *villages* in this region. English is spoken, and their Museum of Wine Growers Implements is worth a look.

From Chateauneuf, take the D192 to **COURTHEZON** then the D977 to **VIOLES**, a pretty ride eastward towards the hills where some of the 16 Rhone wine *villages* are scattered. The most unique one is **BEAUMES DE VENISE** (AOC) where the Muscat grape is used to make a sensuous sweet wine of the Sauternes tradition. Turn right at Violes through **VACQUEYRAS**. Then head north through **GIGONDAS** (AOC), **SABLET** and **SEGURET**. These are red wine towns, with Grenache the primary grape variety.

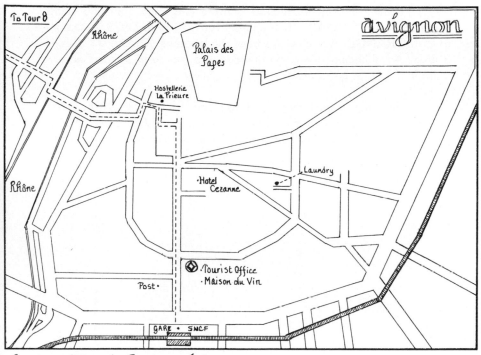

Courtesy: Office de Tourisme Avignon

If the climb up to Seguret is more challenge than you want, continue north to **ROAIX**, then sharply turn left onto D975, a straight road to **ORANGE**. A favorite resort of the Romans, this city still uses its Roman Amphitheatre for performances and has kept Julius Caesar's triumphal arch in good repair.

The train from Orange to Lyon and Tour 9 follows the river, passing through the northern Cotes du Rhone areas of Hermitage (AOC), St. Joseph (AOC) and Cote Rotie (AOC). It's a small mountainous region you might want to explore on your own.

Courtesy: Père Anselme.

The Symbol of the Cotes-du-Rhone.

Maceration Carbonique

Carbonic maceration is a clever technique for fermenting the grapes while they are still inside their skins. This gives maximum fruity flavors. The grapes are left whole, as much as possible and a blanket of innert gas (CO2) prevents air from contaminating the process. The cuve is then pressed and the fermentation finished in the normal way.

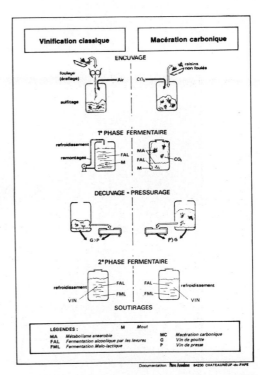

75

8

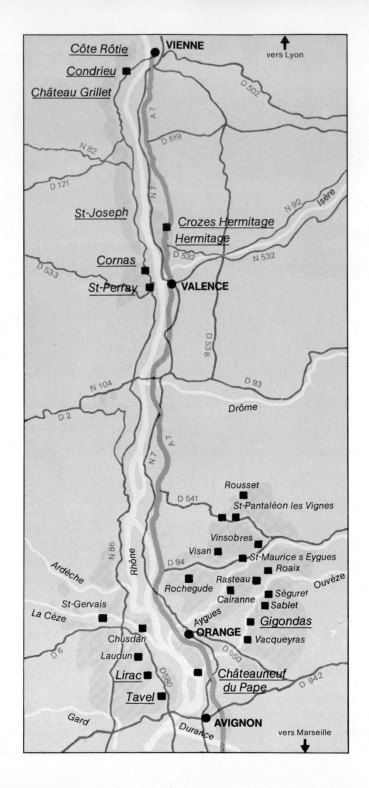

Côte Rôtie
VIENNE
vers Lyon
Condrieu
Château Grillet
D 502
A 7
N 82
D 519
D 121
N 7
St-Joseph
Crozes Hermitage
Hermitage
Cornas
D 532
N 532
D 533
Isère
N 92
St-Perray
VALENCE
D 538
N 104
D 93
D 2
Drôme
N 7
A 7
Rousset
D 541
St-Pantaléon les Vignes
Vinsobres
Visan
N 86
Rhône
D 94
St-Maurice s Eygues
Roaix
Rasteau
Rochegude
Ouvèze
Ardèche
Cairanne
Séguret
Sablet
St-Gervais
Aygues
Gigondas
La Cèze
ORANGE
Chusdan
Vacqueyras
Laudun
D 6
D 950
Lirac
D 580
Châteauneuf
du Pape
D 942
Tavel
Gard
Durance
AVIGNON
vers Marseille

Details & Contacts

TERRAIN: A few river bluffs to pull up, but nothing insurmountable. Wind can be major factor, from the north. IGN #59, 60 (#51 for Hermitage). Distance: 45 kms.

AOC: COTES DU RHONE, COTES DU RHONE VILLAGES, TAVEL, LIRAC, CHATEAUNEUF DU PAPE, GIGONDAS, RASTEAU, MUSCAT BEAUMES DE VENISE, SEGURET, SABLET, VAQUERAS.

MAJOR GRAPES: (red & rosé) Grenache, Syrah, Cinsault, Mourvedre, Carignane, Picpoul. (whites) Clairette, Bourboulenc, Picardan.

FOOD & LODGING: Hotel Cezanne, 11 rue Bancasse, 84000 Avignon. 90.86.34.11.
Hostellerie le Prieure, 7 place du Chapitre, 84000 Avignon. 90.25.18.20. †
Auberge de Tavel, Voie Romaine, 84126 Tavel. 66.50.03.41 (Feb.) †
Hostellerie du Chateau de Cubieres. 84 Cubieres. 66.50.14.28 (Nov. 15-30, Feb. 20-Mar. 20) †
Hotel les Florets, 84190 Gigondas, 90.65.85.01. (Jan-Feb 10) †

CHAMBRES D'HOTE: M. Jamet, Ile de la Bathelasse, 84000 AVIGNON, 90.86.16.74.
Mme. Alfonsina, 5 rue Porte Rouge, 84230 CHATEAUNEUF-DU-PAPE, 90.39.70.20.
M. Francis Marseille, Route du Plan, 84350 COURTHEZON, 90.70.72.85.
M. Fert, "Les Templiers" Les Monts de Chevailong, SABLET, 90.36.94.77.
Mme. Mouret, La Souleiado, SABLET, 90.36.90.66.
M. Vigneron, Cammassot St. Vincent, SABLET, 90.36.94.02.
M. Gourjon, VIOLES, 90.70.92.40.
M. Jouven, St. Guenin, SEGUERET, 90.36.91.31.

CAMPING: Camping Bagatelle, Barthelasse Ile, AVIGNON 90.83.30.39. Open all year.
Colline St. Eutrope, Montee des Princes d'Orange. NASSAN. 90.34.09.22. (Nov.-Feb.)

AJ: Chemin de la Fignasse, 84800 Fontaine-De Vaucluse. 90.20.31.65.

BICYCLE REPAIRS: At Avignon, Orange.

WINERY CONTACTS: Office de Tourisme et Maison du Vin, 41 Cours Jean-Jaures, 84000 Avignon. 90.82.65.11.
Comite Interprofessionnel des Vins des Cotes du Rhone, M. R. Barrelet, (address above), BP 3, 84000 Avignon. 90.86.47.09.
Les Vignerons de Tavel, Route de la Commanderie, 30126 Tavel. 66.50.03.57.
Pere Anselme, 84230 Chateauneuf du Pape. 90.83.70.07.
Clos du Papes, M. Paul Avril, 84230 Chateauneuf du Pape.
Dom. au Vieux Telegraphie, M. Brunier, Route de Chateauneuf du Pape, 84370 Bedarrides. 90.39.01.19.
Domaine de Beaurenard, M. Paul Coulon, 84230 Chateauneuf du Pape.
Les Celliers Amadieu, M. Pierre Amadieu, 84190 Gigondas. 90.65.84.08.

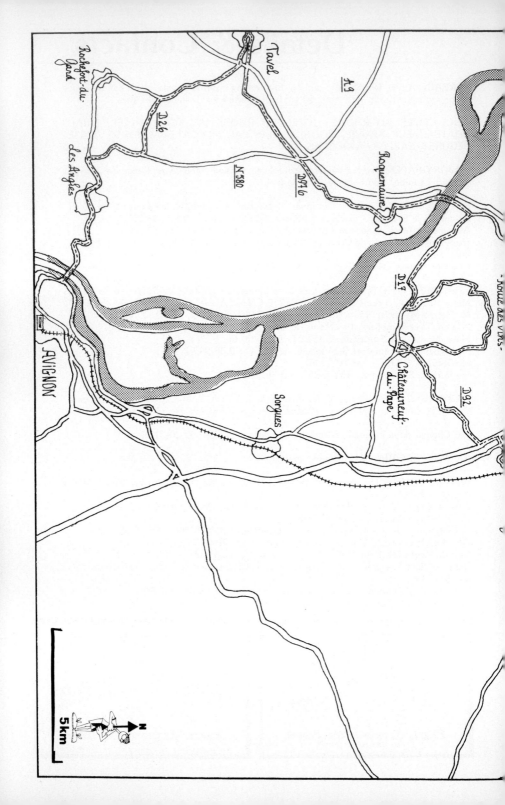

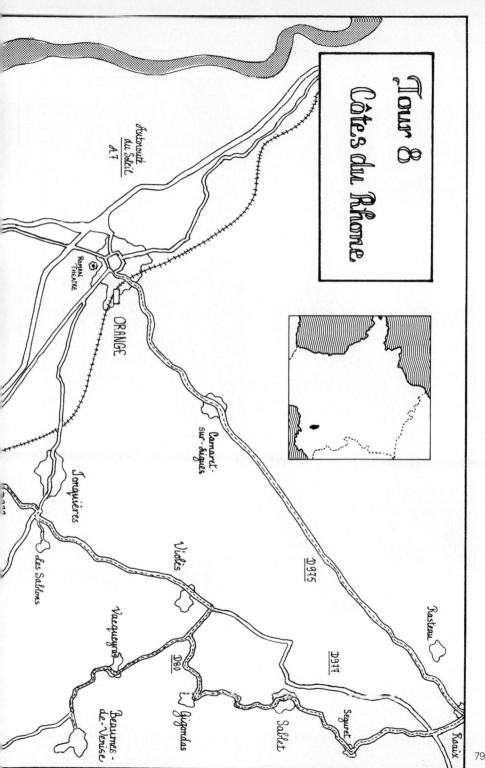

Tour 8
Côtes du Rhône

Autoroute
du Soleil
A7

ROMAN
THEATRE

ORANGE

Camaret-
sur-Aigues

Jonquières

Les Sablons

Violès

Vacqueyras

D80

Beaumes-
de-Venise

Gigondas

Sablet

D975

D977

Rasteau

Seguret

Roaix

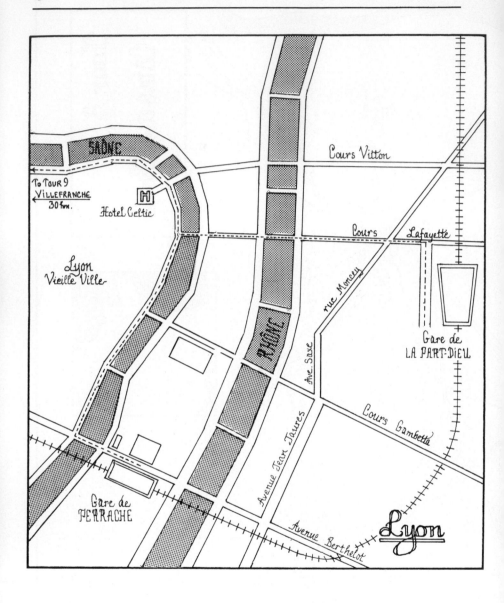

When it rains, taste wine. When it shines, taste wine.

Beaujolais   Tour

Keep Those Reds Rolling Along 9

Beaujolais…rolling hills covered with vineyards and scattered with tiny stone villages from the 17th century…takes the carefree rider up and down a series of easy roller-coaster rides. None challenge beyond pleasure and each rise brings a new wine discovery and a brisk descent.

From **LYON**, follow the west bank of the river on the D51 towards **VILLEFRANCHE**, about 30 kms. You pass the restaurant of Paul Bocuse, and at **ANSE**, the 55,000 acres of the Beaujolais begin. Little Gamay Beaujolais vines in chalky soil announce the *Pays des Pierres Dorees*, the land of the golden stones. This southern end of the district, whose wines are labeled Beaujolais (AOC) and Beaujolais Superieur (AOC) also produce most of the Beaujolais Nouveau (AOC). The better wines are in the *villages* further north.

VILLEFRANCHE is the commercial center of the Beaujolais, but not its inspiration. Continue north towards **ARNAS** and **ST. JULIEN**, and the 39 *Beaujolais Villages*. The small roads are eminently bicyclable…and many of the little villages offer great French country cooking. Look for the town church at noontime, and good food will be close by. There is no major city, and you will probably get "lost" in the maze of small roads, but just keep the names of a few towns in mind, and meander through this lovely countryside in a general northerly direction, stopping to taste as you are inspired. All is quite informal here.

From **ST. JULIEN**, follow signs to **SALLES** and **ST. ETIENNE**. The little Gamay vines find more difficult soils, now (viticultural sadism, again). They are head pruned, *Gobelet*. No wire trellis support is allowed for the hearty Beaujolais Village (AOC). Each of these villages has its unique version and nine have *cru* status. Remember the "growths" of Bordeaux? Here in Burgundy, each village gets the honor, instead of each vineyard. Almost every village has a *degustation* center.

Mt. Brouilly will loom ahead at **ODENAS**, the vineyards of the Cote de Brouilly (AOC) and Brouilly (AOC) cru. Turn right towards **ST. LAGER** to avoid the mountain, but note that the vines climb right to the top, to the chapel of *Notre Dame du Raisin*, Our Lady of the Grape.

From St. Lager to **CERCIE**, cross the major road and stop at the Ardieres River for a swim. It's a stone's throw to the local Mercedes Benz shop. These Beaujolais villagers aren't the *paysan* they appear to be. Nearly 4000 growers make a comfortable living from vineyards of only a few acres each. Once part of the great estate of the Duke of Burgundy, the Beaujolais was divided up among the villagers after the French Revolution and many chateaux were destroyed. Wine survives the vicissitudes of politics.

On to **MORGON** (AOC), now, and then **VILLIE MORGON**, where there is a fine hotel and the hill gets a bit steeper. In **FLEURIE** (AOC), note the roses on the end of each row of vines. These warn the winemaker of drought or disease in his vineyard. Roses are slightly less tolerant than grapevines to catastrophy, so they succumb first.

At **MOULIN-A-VENT** (AOC) and **CHENAS** the vines begin to change from Gamay to the taller, more elegant Chardonnay. The white wines of Pouilly Fuissé (AOC) begin. These are a good hint of the more elegant red and white wines to come, further north in the Burgundy's Cote d'Or.

From **ST. AMOUR** go behind the hills to **CHASSELAS** and **SOLUTRÉ**. Stop at the prehistoric museum here. The soils of this region are strewn with small, flat white pebbles called *chailles*. **POUILLY** (AOC) and **FUISSÉ** (AOC) are on hillier terrain, but these are the last climbs before **MACON** only 10 kms. east.

To skip Macon and continue north, take the pretty country lane from **PRISSÉ** to **LA ROCHE-VINEUSE** and **VERZÉ**. It's 65 kms. to the elite Cote d'Or, the land of the Pinot Noir. At **IGÉ**, 2.5 km beyond Verzé, is an elegant chateau-hotel to restore the weary body, at some expense to the purse. See Tour 10 for how to get to Chagny.

For a good steak sandwich, order "faux filet", with a piece of bread, fries and hot mustard. Quick food, to go.

TERRAIN: Hilly but happy. Wind from the south. IGN Maps #43, 44. Distance: Tours Villefranche 36 km., Villefranche-Macon, 50 km.

AOC: BEAUJOLAIS, BEAUJOLAIS SUPERIEUR, BEAUJOLAIS VILLAGES, BROUILLY, COTE DE BROUILLY, CHENAS, FLEURIE, JULIENAS, MORGON, MOULIN-A-VENT, SAINT AMOUR, CHIROUBLES, POUILLY-FUISSÉ, MACON, MACON SUPERIEUR, MACON-VILLAGES.

GRAPES: Gamay Beaujolais, Chardonnay.

FOOD & LODGING: Paul Bocuse Restaurant, on D51 north of Lyon, Collonges au Mont d'Or. 78.22.01.40. †
Hotel Celtic, Place St. Paul, 69005 Lyon. 78.28.01.12.
Chateau de Chervinges, (HR), 69400 Villefranche. 78.65.29.76. †
Auberge du Cep restaurant, 69820 Fleurie. 74.04.10.77.
Chateau de la Barge, (HR) 71680 Creche sur Soane. 85.37.12.04. †
Hotel du Chateau d'Igé. 71960 Igé, 85.33.33.99. (Nov.-Mar., Thurs. am) †

CHAMBRES D'HOTE: Info in Lyon, 4 place Gensoul, 69002 Lyon. 78.42.65.92.
Mme. Durieu, Le Manoir des Carrieres, 69640 DENICÉ, 74.67.32.99.
Mme. Claude Martin, Domaine le Pave, ST. LAGER, 69220 Belleville-sur-Soane. 74.66.14.62.
Jullien de Pommerol, "Les Brureaux", CHENAS, 69840 Julienas. 78.37.17.40, or 85.36.71.01.
Paul Audras, HAUTE-COMBE, 69840 Julienas. 74.04.41.09.
Michel Bourquart, "Les Tournets", 69840 Julienas. 74.04.43.92.

AJ: Lyon-Venissieux, 51 rue Roger Salengro, 69200 Vinissieux. 78.76.39.23.

CAMPING: DARDILLY (9 km. NW of Lyon), take La Garde exit of A6. 78.35.27.05. Open all year.
At VILLEFRANCHE, CM de la Plage, rte de Riottier. 74.65.33.48. (Sept.29-April 26).

At CLUNY, Foyer Rural Camping, 71250 Cluny. 85.59.05.34.

WINERY CONTACTS: Compagnons du Beaujolais (UIVB), 210 Blvd. Vermorel, 69400 Villefranche. 74.65.45.55.
Pascale Dominique Bouillard-Didier, "La Commune", 69830 Odenas. 74.03.40.30.
Serge Gay, 69910 Villié-Morgon. 74.04.24.78. †
Chateau de Fuissé, M. Marcel Vincent, 71960 Pierre des Clos. 85.37.61.44. †
Mommessin, La Grange St. Pierre, 71009 Macon. 85.34.47.74. †

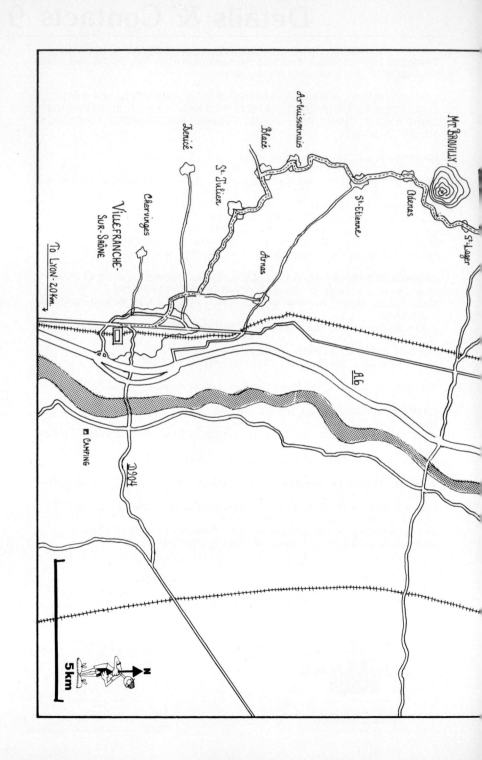

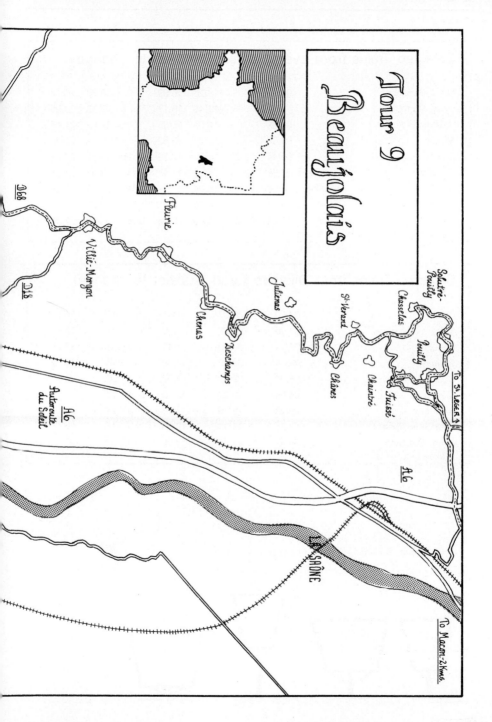

Tour 9

Beaujolais

D68

Fleurie

Villié-Morgon

D18

Chénas

Deschamps

Juliénas

St-Vérand

Chânes

Solutré-
Pouilly

Chasselas

Pouilly

Chaintré

Fuissé

Autoroute
du Soleil

A6

A6

LA SAÔNE

To St Léger

To Mâcon-2Kms.

Selected Trains from Lyon to Dijon (subject to change)

Lyon (Perrache)		08:12		13:26	16:09		18:22	20:47
Lyon (Part-Dieu)				13:45	16:17		18:33	20:55
Villefranche		08:39		14:05	16:35		18:52	21:13
Mâcon		09:05		14:29	16:58		19:11	21:36
Chalon-sur-Söane		09:44	12:23*	15:00	17:36	18:15*	19:42	22:09
Chagny	09:28*	09:55	12:44	15:12	17:47	18:33	19:53	22:18
Beaune	09:40	10:06	13:00	15:24	17:57	18:45	20:03	22:28
Nuits St. Georges		10:17	13:17	18:06	18:55		22:37	
Dijon .		10:00	10:32	13:39	15:45	18:19	19:10	20:22	22:49

*Takes bicycles *a main*.

Selected Trains from Dijon to Lyon (subject to change)

Dijon	07:40	09:07	11:21	15:45	17:23*
Nuits St. Georges	07:55	09:20	11:36		17:42
Beaune	08:04	09:29	11:45	16:05	17:56
Chagny	08:14	09:40	11:55	16:16	18:12
Chalon-sur-Söane	08:26	09:57	12:07	16:28	18:29
Mâcon	09:04	10:27	12:40	17:02	
Villefranche	09:28	10:49	12:58	17:24	
Lyon (Part-Dieu)		11:11	13:18	17:43	
Lyon (Perrache)	09:47	11:19	13:26	17:53	

*Takes bicycles *a main*.

The Gobelet "ascending" theory of pruning.

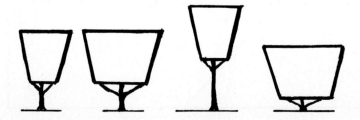

Burgundy   Tour

Cote de Beaune   **10**

From **MACON** north to the Cote Chalonnaise, there is a low range of mountains to cross. Best bicycle pass for this is: northwest towards **(LA ROCHE VINEUSE)** on the N79, cutting off at **CHEVAGNY** to **VERZÉ**, through the Maconnais.

From Verse' go to **IGE** then to **AZE** on the D85, then take the pass towards **(DONZY)**. Turn right as you reach the top of the ridge, to **BLANOT, CHISSEY LES MACONS** and **CORMATIN**. At the D981, turn right towards **BUXY** and the beginning of the Cote Chalonnaise. No more hills from here all the way to Dijon, the north end of the Bourgogne!

This is the Maconnais (AOC), red wines made from the Gamay grape. The white wines, made with Chardonnay, are White Burgundy (AOC). At Montagny (AOC) it becomes the Cote Chalonnaise (AOC), with reds from the great Burgundian grape, Pinot Noir. The whites, from the Aligote, are Bourgogne Alicote (AOC), unless specified by one of the many smaller AOC. The Passe-Tout-Grains (AOC) is a blend of Pinot Noir and Gamay.

The autoroute to the east through Chalon-sur-Soane leaves the D981 peaceful. At the major crossroads beyond **GERMOLLES**, go left on the D978 to **MERCUREY** (AOC), a happy series of *vignerons* along the road with plenty of opportunity to taste both whites and reds. There is a back road through town north that returns to the D981.

Just before **CHAGNY**, climb up through the vineyards to Domaine de la Folie. In Chagny, the three-star restaurant, Lameloise, offers another chance to experience that specifically French ailment, *crise de foie*, a revolt of the liver from too much rich food. It feels something like a bad hangover, and the only anti-dote is more cycling.

Use your water bottle as a wine decanter, if you want to drink demurely.
No restaurant in France will let you bring your own wine bottle.

From Chagny follow the N6 north briefly to **CORPEAU**, a right fork that allows a quiet happy route to **PULIGNY-MONTRACHET** (AOC) and **MEURSAULT** (AOC) a few minutes away. There are 19 acres in Montrachet, and over a dozen different owners; some have only a few rows of vines, but they are worth their weight in gold. This is part of the *Cote d'Or*, called the *Cote de Beaune*. The *Grand Vins* are here, made from the great Pinot Noir.

Burgundy is France's most popular wine region, yet it remains peaceful and friendly. Still, as the wines of this area increase in value without any possibility of increasing in quantity, their makers are retiring to a more private world. As in the Bordeaux, stop in wherever you see the welcome signs, *degustation* and *vente directe*, but call or write ahead to the others.

There are three different classifications of fine Cote d'Or wines: the *Grand Cru*, identified by the name of the vineyard only; the *Premiere Cru*, first labeled with the name of the village, then with the name of the vineyard; and the *Village* wines, only named by their village. As usual, the more specific the label identification, the more rigidly-controlled the wine.

The road through Meursault, famous for its dry, white Chardonnay, leads back to the village of **AUXEY-DURESSES** (AOC), a comparative bargain among the fine wines of this region. From there, climb the small rise to **VOLNAY** (AOC) and **POMMARD** (AOC), more big names in Burgundy, with heady wines and manicured vineyard rows. The vineyards continue right up to the edge of historic old **BEAUNE**, on the D981. Here, you'll find a wide selection of hotels, a bike shop, a laundromat, and a town dedicated to wine.

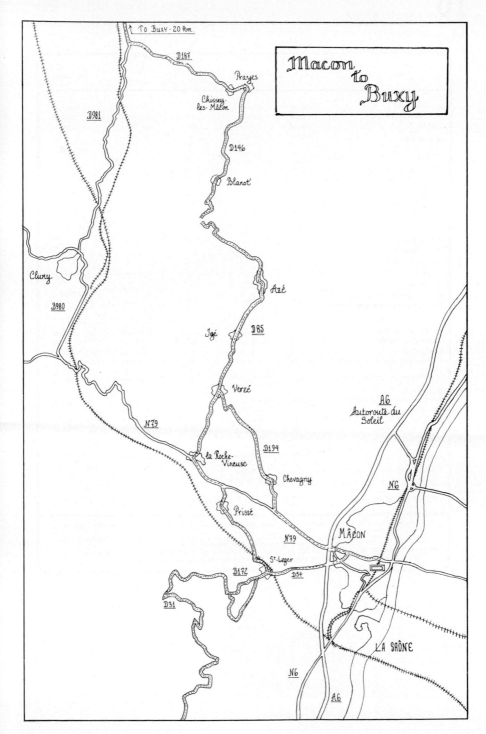

To Buxy - 20 Km.

D187

Prayes

Chissey-les-Mâcon

D146

Blanot

D981

Azé

Cluny

Igé   D85

D1980

Verzé

A6
Autoroute du
Soleil

N79

D194

la Roche-Vineuse

Chevagny

N6

Prissé

N79   MÂCON

St-Leger

D172   D54

D31

LA SAÔNE

N6

A6

Macon to Buxy

Appellation	Color	Cépage	Minimum degree sugar	Maximum yield allowed	Annual production
MOULIN-A-VENT	rouge	Gamay	10°	48 hl ha	(*) 16.000 hl
SAINT-AMOUR	rouge	Gamay	10°	48 hl ha	8.000 hl
CHÉNAS	rouge	Gamay	10°	48 hl ha	(*) 3.000 hl
BEAUJOLAIS	rouge	Gamay	9°	55 hl ha	
	blanc	Chardonnay	9°5	55 hl ha	
BEAUJOLAIS SUPÉR. OU VILLAGES	rouge	Gamay	10°	55 hl ha	(*) 30.000 hl
	blanc	Chardonnay	10°5	55 hl ha	
Rendement maximum: 50 pour Beaujolais-Villages rouge.					
POUILLY-FUISSÉ	blanc	Chardonnay	11°	55 hl ha	25.000 hl
POUILLY-VINZELLES					
POUILLY-LOCHÉ					3.000 hl
SAINT-VÉRAN (²)				55	10.000 hl
MACON BLANC	blanc	Chardonnay	10°	65 hl ha	120.000 hl
MACON SUPÉRIEUR	blanc	Chardonnay	11°	65 hl ha	
MACON VILLAGES					
MACON ROUGE	rouge	Gamay	9°	55 hl ha	60.000 hl
MACON SUPÉRIEUR	rouge	Gamay	10°	55 hl ha	
MACON (assorti du nom de la commune)					
BOURGOGNE BLANC	blanc	Chardonnay	10°5	68 hl ha	(*) 5.000 hl
BOURGOGNE ROUGE	rouge	Pinot noir	10°	55 hl ha	(*) 25.000 hl
BOURGOGNE ALIGOTÉ	blanc	Aligoté	9°5	68 hl ha	(*) 20.000 hl
BOURGOGNE GRAND ORDINAIRE ..	rouge	Gamay	9°	55 hl ha	(*) 8.000 hl
BOURGOGNE PASSE-TOUT-GRAINS..	rouge	Assemblage de 1/3 Pinot noir et 2/3 Gamay	9°5	55 hl ha	(*) 25.000 hl
BOURGOGNE HAUTES COTES DE BEAUNE (²)	rouge	Pinot noir	10°	hl ha	(*) 3.500 hl
MONTAGNY	blanc	Chardonnay	11°	50 hl ha	3.000 hl
GIVRY	blanc	Chardonnay	11°	45 hl ha	300 hl
	rouge	Pinot	10°5	45 hl ha	2.000 hl
RULLY	blanc	Chardonnay	11°	50 hl ha	1.200 hl
	rouge	Pinot	10°5	40 nl ha	500 hl
MERCUREY	blanc	Chardonnay	11°	45 hl ha	800 hl
	rouge	Pinot	10°5	40 hl ha	15.000 hl
CRÉMANT DE BOURGOGNE (³)	blanc	Chardonnay Aligoté et Pinot	8°5	*10.500 KGS ha*	—
COTE DE BEAUNE VILLAGES	blanc	Chardonnay	11°	55 hl ha	(*) 4.000 hl
	rouge	Pinot	10°5	40 hl ha	

(*) Volume de la récolte en Saône-et-Loire, qui ne correspond pas au volume total de l'appellation, laquelle est récoltée également sur d'autres départements.

(*1) Il s'agit du rendement de base relatif à l'appellation en cause. Ce rendement peut être modifié annuellement par décision de l'I.N.A.O. homologuée par arrêté du ministre de l'Agriculture, il est alors dénommé rendement annuel.

(2) Pour avoir droit à ces appellations, les vins issus du vignoble délimité doivent obtenir l'agrément d'une commission de dégustation.

(3) Conditions de production du vin de base semblables à celles du champagne : dégustation obligatoire.

Domaine du Chateau de Meursault.

TERRAIN: Gentle rolls, with a wind from the south. IGN Maps #44 and #37. Distance: Macon to Beaune, 100 kms.

AOC: BOURGOGNE (Burgundy), CHALON, MACON, COTES DE BEAUNE, HAUTES COTES DE BEAUNE, GIVRY, MERCUREY, RULLY, CHASSAGNE-MONTRACHET, PULIGNY-MONTRACHET, MEURSAULT, AUXEY-DURESSES, VOLNAY, POMMARD, BEAUNE.

GRAPES: Gamay Noir, Aligote, Pinot Noir, Chardonnay.

FOOD & LODGING: Chateau d'Hote, Soane et Loire, Blvd. Henri-Durant, 71000 Macon. 85.38.50.66.
Hotel-Restaurant Lameloise, 37 Place d'Armes, 71150 Chagny. 85.87.08.85. †
Hostellerie du Chateau de Bellecroix, 71150 Chagny (on N6 2 kms S. of Chagny). 85.87.13.86. (Wed., 20 Dec. — 1 Feb.)
Hotellerie du Val d'Or, Grandreue-Givry, 71640 Mercurey. 85.47.13.70. † (Sept.1-15; Dec. 15-31).
Hotel des Roches, SAINT ROMAIN, 21190 Meursault. 80.21.21.63.
La Bouzerotte Bistrot, 21200 Bouze-les Beaune. 80.22.52.53. (Mon. Tues., August).

CHAMBRES D'HOTE: Mme. Noelle Martin, CISSEY-MERCEUIL, 21190 Meursault. 80.21.47.39.

CAMPING: At CHAGNY, rue du Paquier (contact Syndicat). At MEURSAULT: Camping de la Grappe d'Or, Pre de Manche, 80.21.22.48. (Nov.-Mar.)
At BEAUNE: Camp Municipal des Cent Vignes, Rue Auguste, Dubois (at D2 towards Savigny). 80.22.03.81. (Nov.-Mar.)

AJ: rue d'Amsterdam, 71100 CHALON-SUR-SOANE. 85.46.62.77. (Dec.15-Jan.15)

WINERY CONTACTS: Comite Interprofessional des Vins de Bourgogne et Macon (CIVB), Maison du Tourisme, Ave. du Marechal De Lattre de Tassigny, 71000 Macon. 85.38.20.15.
Michel Juillot, viticulteur, Mercurey, 71640 Givry. 80.45.27.27.
Domaine de la Folie, M. Noel-Bouton, 71150 Chagny-en-Bourgogne. 80.83.18.59.
Domaine Bernard Delagrange, Meursault. vente directe.
La Pousse d'Or, M. Gerard Potel, Volnay, 21190 Meursault. 80.22.10.73.
Domaine du Chateau de Meursault, Meursault. 80.21.22.98. Open daily.
Jean Monnier et son fils, Meursault. 80.21.21.92.

BICYCLE REPAIRS: In Macon and Beaune.

The back roads of France are heaven for cyclists.

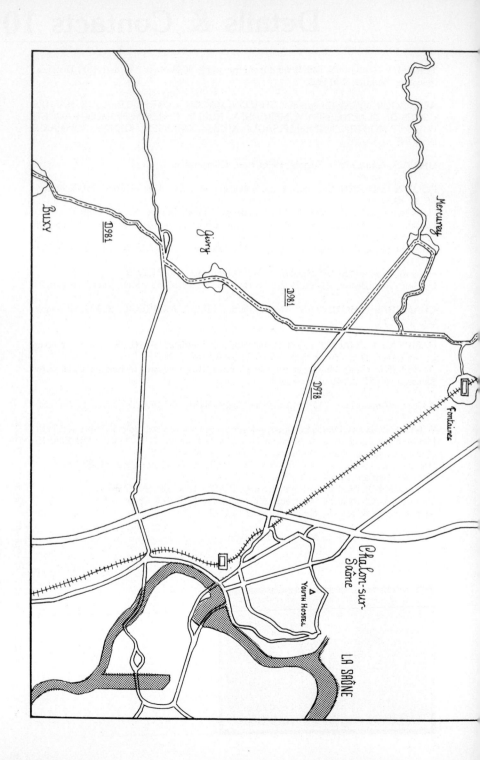

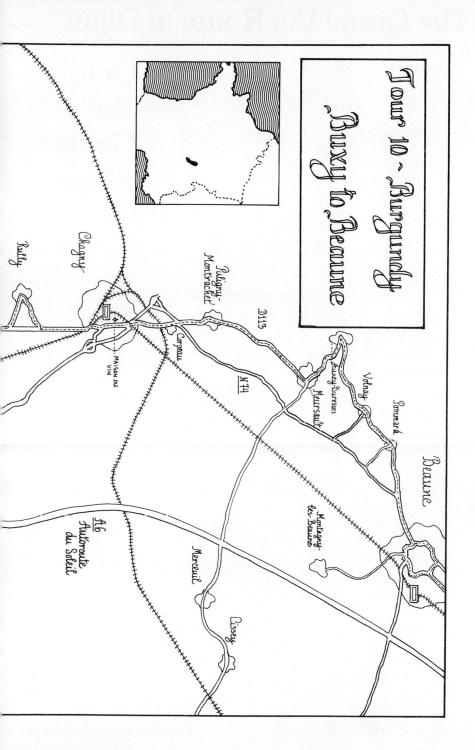

Tour 10 ~ Burgundy
Buxy to Beaune

Rully

Chagny

Puligny-Montrachet

Corpeau

MAISON DU VIN

D113

N74

Buxy-Duresses

Volnay

Meursault

Pommard

Beaune

Montigny-lès-Beaune

A6
Autoroute
du Soleil

Merceuil

Bissey

The Grand Vin Route to Dijon

Onto the Golden Slope

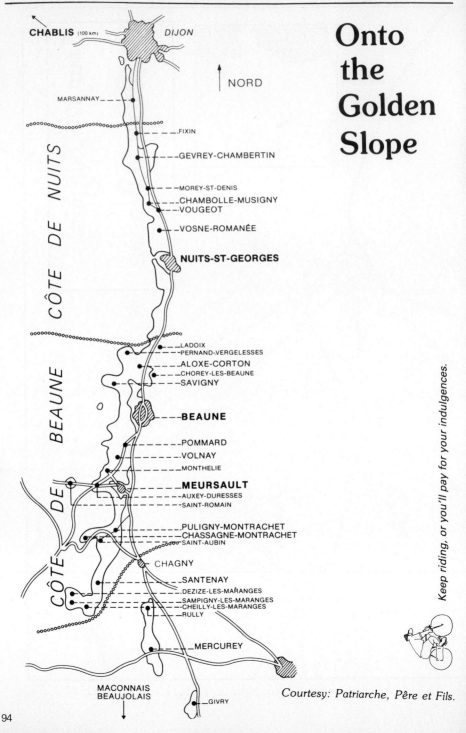

CHABLIS (100 km)   DIJON

NORD

MARSANNAY

FIXIN

GEVREY-CHAMBERTIN

MOREY-ST-DENIS
CHAMBOLLE-MUSIGNY
VOUGEOT

VOSNE-ROMANÉE

NUITS-ST-GEORGES

CÔTE DE NUITS

LADOIX
PERNAND-VERGELESSES
ALOXE-CORTON
CHOREY-LES-BEAUNE
SAVIGNY

BEAUNE

POMMARD
VOLNAY
MONTHELIE

MEURSAULT
AUXEY-DURESSES
SAINT-ROMAIN

PULIGNY-MONTRACHET
CHASSAGNE-MONTRACHET
SAINT-AUBIN

CÔTE DE BEAUNE

CHAGNY

SANTENAY
DEZIZE-LES-MARANGES
SAMPIGNY-LES-MARANGES
CHEILLY-LES-MARANGES
RULLY

MERCUREY

MACONNAIS
BEAUJOLAIS

GIVRY

Keep riding, or you'll pay for your indulgences.

Courtesy: Patriarche, Père et Fils.

94

Cote de Nuits

Historic old Beaune offers many an opportunity to taste. For example, Patriarche, on the north side of the old walled town, allows you to taste over 20 different wines of the Bourgogne, for a small fee. Wander in their candlelit caves, from barrel to barrel. The *sommellier* on hand will be able to answer all of your questions, often in English. Beaune is riddled with these underground caves, and several producers offer the opportunity to see them and compare the products of the various years and villages.

Back on the road north from **BEAUNE** take the N. 74 towards **NUITS-ST. GEORGES** and cut off to the left on the D. 18 for (**SAVIGNY-LES-BEAUNE**). Stay on the D. 18 to **PERNAND VERGELESSES**, then cut to the right to **MAGNY-LES-VILLERS**.

This avoids the main thoroughfare. Continue to **VILLERS-LA-FAYE** then right again to **CHAUX**. Take the D. 8 descent into **NUITS-ST.-GEORGES** (AOC).

Now, you are in the Cotes de Nuits, which started at Corgoloin. Follow the main route north to **VOSNE-ROMANEE** (AOC) and turn left, mounting the hill to the *Route des Grands Vins*, a beautiful meander from village to village above the valley floor, passing through 20-odd *Grand Cru* villages, some of the world's most famous and expensive Pinot Noir.

Each village has an international fan club on this route: Nuits St. Georges, **VOUGEOT** (AOC), **MOREY ST. DENIS** (AOC), **GEVREY-CHAMBERTIN** (AOC), **FIXIN** (AOC).

History abounds here. For instance, Clos Vougeot is home of the *Chevaliers du Tastevins*, the hallowed promotional society of the Burgundy whose gourmet feasts are world famous. The vineyards around the chateau were planted in 1098 AD! The Vougeot vineyard has 125 acres and 66 owners.

Few wineries here offer spontaneous tastings of their rare and expensive commodity. Check the "Details" section for contacts, and call ahead, or keep your eyes peeled for *Degustations*.

The road wanders in less than 20 kms. into **DIJON**, the mustard capital. Watch carefully for the signs to *Gare Dijon-ville* where regular *TGV* service zips you to Paris in two hours. There is conventional service, as well, from Dijon to Epernay, and Tour 12, the Champagne.

VRAY PORTRAICT DE LA VILLE DE BEAVLNE (1574)

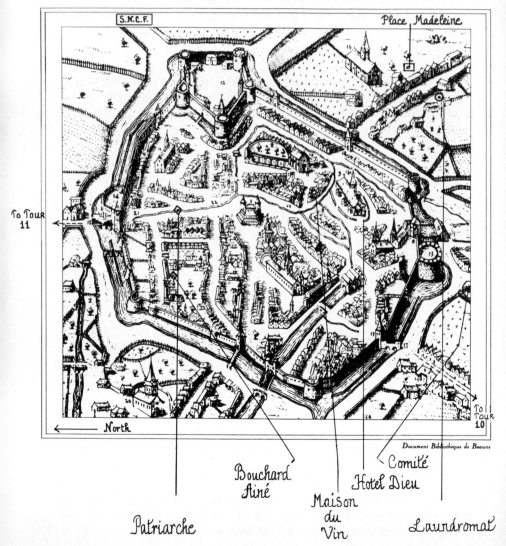

Document Bibliothèque de Beaune

TERRAIN: Short pull up to the wine road. IGN Map #37. Distance: 38 kms.

AOC: BOURGOGNE (Burgundy), COTES DE NUIT, HAUTES COTES DE NUITS, BEAUNE, CHOREY LES BEAUNE, ALOXE-CORTON, NUITS-ST. GEORGES, VOSNE-ROMANEE, VOUGEOT, CHAMBOLLE-MUSIGNY, MOREY-SAINT-DENIS, GEVREY-CHAMBERTIN, FIXIN.

GRAPES: Pinot Noir.

FOOD & LODGING: L'Auberge Bourguignonne, 4 pl. Madeleine, 21200 Beaune. 80.22.23.53.
Hotel de la Poste, Blvd. Clemenceau, 21200 Beaune. 80.22.08.11. [†]
Beaun-otel, Ave. Faubourg-Bretannier, Beaune. 80.22.11.01.
Hotel Chez Jeannette, 7 rue Noisot, FIXIN. 21220 Gevrey-Chambertin. 80.52.45.49.

CHAMBRES D'HOTE: Mme. Gisele Thibert, Les Meix de Chevignerot, VIGNOLLES 21200 Beaune. 80.22.27.47.
Mme. Michelle Girard, CHAMBOEUF, 21220 Gevrey-Chambertin. 80.51.81.60.
Genevieve Bartet, Clos St. Jacques, 3 rue Neuve, 21220 Gevrey-Chambertin. 80.51.82.06.
Roger Cluny, 5 rue du Chateau, 21220 Gevrey-Chambertin. 80.34.38.46.
Earnest Vaivrand, MONTAGNY-LES-BEAUNE, 21200 Beaune. 80.22.24.52.
Colette Michaudet, Chemin de l'Argilliere, 21220 Gevrey-Chambertin. 80.34.34.29.

CAMPING: At VOUGEOT: Camp du Moulin. 80.29.16.77. (Oct.-Apr.) At SAVIGNY-LES-BEAUNE, Rt. Bouilland.

AJ: 1 Blvd. Champollion, 21100 DIJON. 80.71.32.12. Open all year.

WINERY CONTACTS: Comite Interprofessional de la Cote d'Or, 11 rue Henri Dunant, BP 168, 21204 Beaune. 80.22.21.35.
Patriarche, Pere et Fils, 5-7 rue du College, 21204 Beaune. 80.22.23.20.
Bouchard, Aine, M. Terry Price, BP 87, 36 rue St. Marguerite, 21203 Beaune. 80.22.07.67.
Reine Pedauque, Porte St. Nicholas, 21200 Beaune. 80.22.23.11. Tours & tasting daily.
Marche aux Vins, just behind the Tourist Office, next to the Hospice. 80.22.27.69.
F. Chauvenet, BP 4, 21700 Nuits-St.-Georges. 80.61.12.11.
Henri Perrot-Minot, 21740 Morey St. Denis. 80.34.32.51.
Domaine Dujac, M. Jacques Seysses, 21740 Morey-St.-Denis. 80.34.32.58.
Philippe Batachi, 11 rue Gaizot, 21220 Gevrey-Chambertin. 80.34.36.01.
Cote d'Or Tourisme, Hotel du Department, BP 1601, 21035 Dijon. 80.73.81.81.

BICYCLE REPAIRS: At Beaune, Dijon.

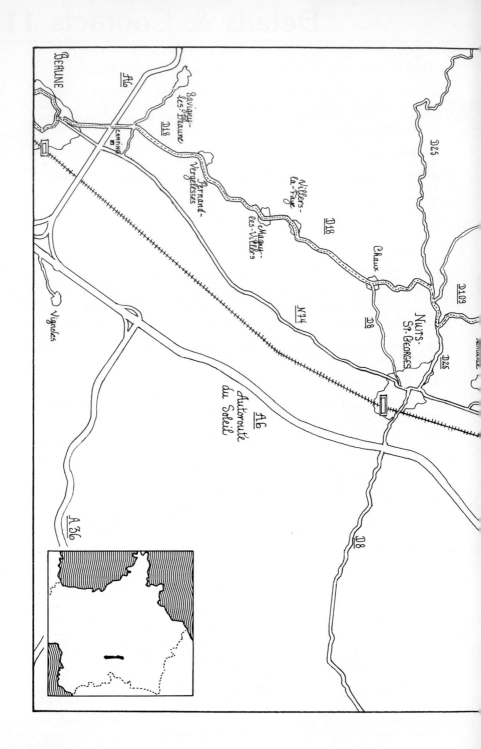

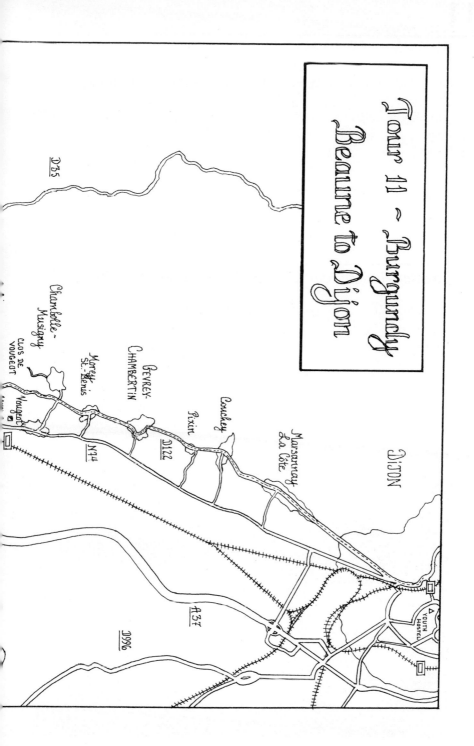

Tour 11 ~ Burgundy
Beaume to Dijon

DIJON

D35

Marsannay
La Côte

Couchey

Pixin

D122

GEVREY-
CHAMBERTIN

Morey
St. Denis

N74

Chambolle-
Musigny

CLOS DE
VOUGEOT

Vougeot

A37

D996

YOUTH
HOSTEL

Selected Trains from Paris to Lyon (subject to change)

Paris (Gare de Lyon)	08:00†	08:05†	09:40	10:00†	11:00†	12:39	15:00†	12:15†
Dijon		10:06				15:45		
Beaune						16:04		
Chagny						16:14		
Macon			11:12	13:21		16:58		
Villefranche			11:52			17:23		
Lyon (Part-Dieu)	10:02		14:03	12:08	13:02	17:46	17:02	17:25

†TGV

Selected Trains from Lyon to Paris (subject to change)

Lyon (Part-Dieu)	09:25	10:00†	12:00†	13:45†	15:00†	16:17	17:00†	18:33
Villefranche			14:05	14:05		16:36		18:53
Macon	10:02			14:31		17:01		19:13
Chagny				15:15		17:41		19:53
Beaune				15:26		17:57		20:03
Dijon	11:04			15:45		18:19†		20:22†
Paris (Lyon)	13:16	12:00	14:04	18:50	17:04	20:19	19:10	23:33

†TGV

Champagne   Tour

The Right Gas   12

Epernay is home of the stars, in the bubbly business: Moet & Chandon, Mercier, Perrier Jouet, Pol Roger. The Tourist Information Office *Syndicat d'Initiative*, in a gazebo in the park just to the right of the gates to the *gare* as you leave, opens at 10, as does most everything in French country towns.

A tour of Moet & Chandon headquarters, 3 minutes away on the Ave de Champagne, is a fascinating, if chilly, 45-minute introduction to the original *vin mousseaux* wines made in the *methode champenoise*. They walk you through part of the 19 miles of cellars begun in 1720, and continuing today, all dug by hand through the chalk soil so intrinsic to the wines of this region.

Below 8 inches of top soil in the Champagne region lie 1000 feet of chalk, created by shellfish deposits from an ancient seabed. The chalk absorbs heat all summer and releases it through the cold months, helping to protect the Pinot Noir, Pinot Meunier and Chardonnay vines from killing frosts.

The Champagne process *methode champenoise* and the distinctive bottle and cork, were developed by a monk, Dom Perignon just across the river from Epernay in the late 1600s. His original means of disgorging sediments from a second fermentation, while retaining the gas, the evolution of the Champagne bottle which holds the wine at a pressure of 6 atmospheres, and the art of turning the settling bottles are explained in English in the M&C tour. You can sample the wines in the garden as your guide reminisces of Napoleon's happy days there.

When tasting any sparkling wine, note the flavor and the size of the bubbles. Both are indications of quality. Your comparison of the wines here with the *vin mousseux* of the Loire Valley and the *cremant* of Burgundy will be interesting. All use the *methode champenoise*, but only this region and these grapes can make "Champagne". It's one of the few wines that really should be drunk chilled.

More guided tours and tunnels are up the Ave. de Champagne at Perrier Jouet, Pol Roger and Mercier. The wines of this area have been those of kings since 1328.

A taste of champagne will soothe a biker's budget.

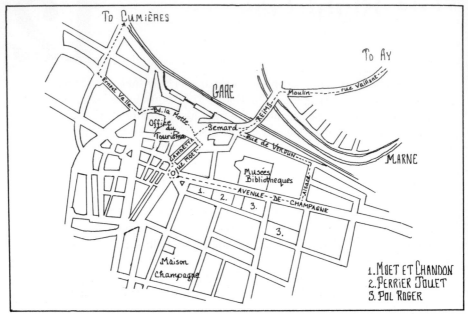

Epernay

To get out to the grapes, return to the *Syndicat* and follow the road behind it to **CUMIERES** passing the campground. Cross the Marne River and the vineyards begin. There are numerous less famous producers beginning at Cumieres, where Champagne Marniquet will offer a friendly glass of their best *Brut*, once roused from their work in various corners of the winery.

Brut, Extra Sec, Sec, and *Demi-Sec (Doux)* are the typical choices, driest to sweetest, which the law defines. The less sweet the Champagne, the finer the blend of wine *cuvee* from which it is made, and the higher price.

Follow D1 west (left) to **DAMERY**, and then right at the stop sign. The road goes to **FLEURY-LA-RIVIERE**, a slow climb into a lovely vineyard-covered valley. Chardonnay and Pinot Noir cling rather pitifully to the chalky hillsides. Fleury has several small *ventes directes*.

Dom Perignon.

Descend towards **ROMERY**, crossing the valley in a zip and then climb to the forest plateau, the *Parc Naturel de la Montagne de Reims*.

Listen for the cuckoo birds as you descend again into **HAUTVILLERS**, with the lovely old Norman abbey, now a shrine to Dom Perignon. He arrived here as cellarmaster in 1668 and is buried inside.

Follow the signs towards **DIZY** to the Marne River valley, and **AY**, on the D1 again. The peaceful canal dug to straighten the twisting route of the Marne has wine cellars all along the way, which still use this shipping route. The villages become smaller as the D1 goes east through **MAREUIL-SUR-AY, BISSEUIL** and **TOURS-SUR-MARNE**, home of Laurent-Perrier.

At Tours-sur-Marne there is an excellent country inn, La Touraine Champenoise, tucked back in the village on the canal's bank.

Follow D1 west (left) to **DAMERY**, and then turn right at the stop sign. The road goes to **FLEURY-LA-RIVIERE**, a slow climb into a lovely vineyard-covered valley. Chardonnay and Pinot Noir cling rather pitifully to the chalky hillsides. Fleury also has several small *ventes directes*.

Leave the D1 for the D19 to **BOUZY**, home of some of the best red and white wines of the region, called the *Coteaux Champenoise* (AOC). Try a Bouzy Rouge or two in this stone village on the windswept plain, the eastern edge of the Champagne.

Now go west towards **TAUXIERES-MUTRY**, an easy rise and a long descent following the Livre river though **FONTAINE-SUR-AY** and **AVENAY**. The hilltop town of Mutigny commands this valley as Hautviller did the Marne. The road follows the railroad tracks back to **AY**, then through **MAGENTA** to **EPERNAY**.

There are actually three distinct districts in Champagne. We've covered the Vallee de la Marne. The Montagne de Reims, to the north, and the Cote des Blancs (AOC) south of Epernay, complete this region: 55,000 beautiful acres in all. The *Syndicat* has a folder of six *promenades* by bicycle, if you want more touring suggestions.

Champagne

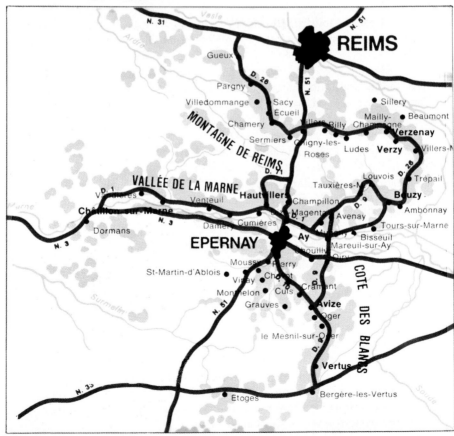

How The Methode Champenoise Works

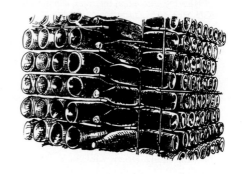

Champenoise

White wines are made in the normal way, then blended by the cellarmaster to the desired *cuvee* and bottled with a certain *dosage* of sugar added, and a crown cap applied.

The bottles lay horizontally for a year or more, going through a slow, cold second fermentation. Gas forms inside the bottle and a sediment of yeast particles drops to the side.

The bottles are then gently mounted on riddling racks, where they are skillfuly turned and raised to increase angles, allowing the sediment to fall over several months' time into the neck of the bottle. A good riddler can move 50,000 bottles a day, and each bottle must be moved several times.

When all the sediment is in the top, it is frozen, the cap popped off ejecting the frozen sediment, and a regular Champagne cork inserted, retaining the gas produced by the second fermentation. A wire encases the cork, and the bottle is then ready to sell. Sparkling wine made from good quality *cuvee* will age in this state for years.

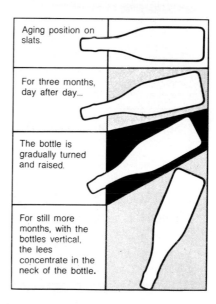

Aging position on slats.	
For three months, day after day...	
The bottle is gradually turned and raised.	
For still more months, with the bottles vertical, the lees concentrate in the neck of the bottle.	

12 Details & Contacts

TERRAIN: Flat along the river, steep climb up to the *Parc*. Prevailing wind from the east. IGN Map #10. Distance: 45 kms.

AOC: CHAMPAGNE, COTEAUX CHAMPENOIS.

GRAPES: Chardonnay, Pinot Noir, Pinot Meunier.

FOOD & LODGING: Le Bar Champetre Grill, rue de l'Aubrois, 51 Hautvillers. 26.59.40.30.
La Touraine Champenoise, 51150 Tours-sur-Marne. 26.59.91.93.
Royal Champagne, 51160 Champillon-Bellevue. 26.51.11.51. † (R&C)

CHAMBRES D'HOTE: M. Jean Rodex, AMBONNAY, 51150 Tours-sur-Marne. 26.57.08.76. (harvest).
M. Jean Marie Tarlant, OEUILLY, 51200 Epernay. 26.58.30.60.

GITES D'ETAPES (even less formal than Chambres d'Hote): M. Barbier, TAUXIERES Mutry, 51160 Ay. 26.59.03.11. (harvest).
M. Brun, 1 impasse Saint-Vincent, 51160 Ay. 26.50.12.73. (harvest)
M. Maizieres, Chemin des Fervins Trepail, 51160 TOURS-SUR-MARNE. 26.59.05.04. (harvest)
M. Gabriel, 22 rue Charles-de-Gaulle, AVENAY-VAL-D'OR, 51160 Ay. 26.52.31.26. (harvest)

AJ: 14-16 rue du Bassin, 51380 VERZY. 26.97.90.10.

CAMPING: Camp Municipal Epernay, (towards Cumieres). 26.51.50.71. (Dec.-Feb.)

BICYCLE REPAIRS: Cycles et Cyclomoteurs, 56 Ave. J. et G. Lecomte, 51200 EPERNAY. 26.54.10.87. Cycles Peugeot, Place Henri Martin, 51160 AY, 26.50.12.44.

WINERY CONTACTS: Comite Interprofessional du Vin de Champagne (CIVC), 5 rue Henri-Martin, BP 135, 51204 Epernay. 26.54.47.20.
Moet & Chandon, 20 ave de Champagne, 51201 Epernay, Tours daily, 10-12, 2-5, (Sundays in summer). 26.51.71.11.
Perrier-Jouet, 24-28, ave de Champagne, 51201 Epernay. 26.51.20.53. Open daily for tours and tasting.
Pol Roger, 1 rue Henri-Lelarge, 51230 Epernay. 26.51.41.95.
Champagne Mercier, 73 ave de Champagne, 51200 Epernay. 26.51.74.74.
Champagne Blosseville-Marniquet, 51200 Cumieres. 26.51.29.70.
Laurent-Perrier, 51150 Tours-sur-Marne. 26.51.23.89.
Delavenne Pere et Fils, 6 rue de Tours, Bouzy, 55150 Tours-sur-Marne. 26.59.02.04.

Selected Trains from Paris to Epernay (subject to change)

Paris (Gare de l'Est)	08:34	11:06	12:47	18:55
Epernay	09:44	12:15	14:00	20:10

Selected Trains from Epernay to Paris (subject to change)

Epernay	09:02	11:30	12:30	16:40	19:00	20:54
Paris (Gare de l'Est)	10:36	12:40	13:55	18:02	20:10	22:05

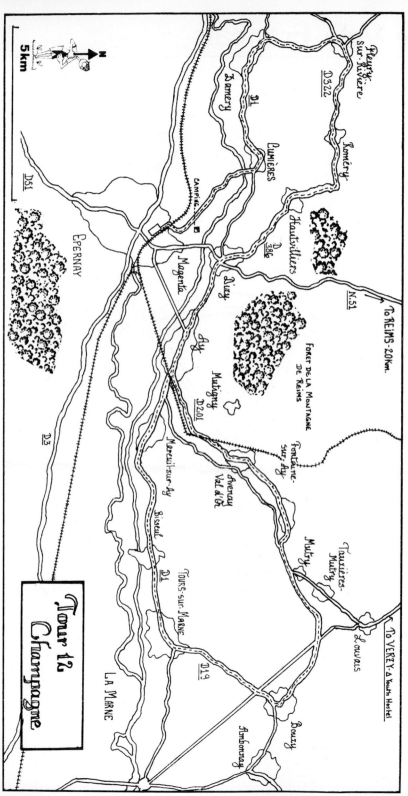

Tour 12
Champagne

N

5km

D322   D51

Fleury-sur-Rivière

Damery

Romery

31

Cumières

Hautvillers

D386

CAMPING.

Dizay

Magenta

ÉPERNAY

Forêt de la Montagne de Reims

Mutigny

D201

Tauxières-Mutry

Fontaine-sur-Ay

To REIMS - 20 km.

N.51

Ay

Avenay Val d'Or

Mareuil-sur-Ay

Bisseul

Louvais

Mutry

To VEREY - & Youth Hostel

Bouzy

D1

Tours-sur-Marne

D3

D19

Ambonnay

LA MARNE

Le Velo Francais

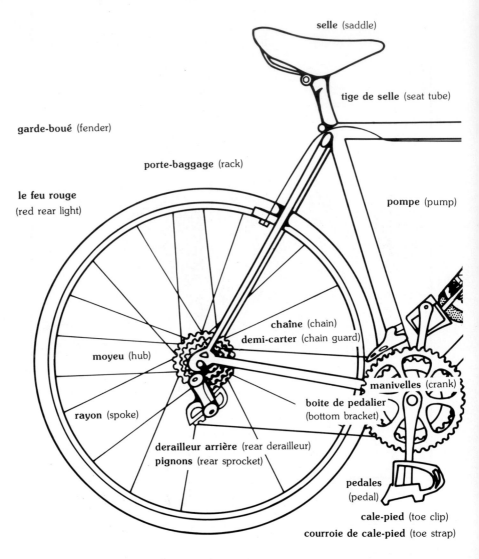

selle (saddle)

tige de selle (seat tube)

garde-boué (fender)

porte-baggage (rack)

le feu rouge
(red rear light)

pompe (pump)

chaîne (chain)
demi-carter (chain guard)

moyeu (hub)

manivelles (crank)

boite de pedalier
(bottom bracket)

rayon (spoke)

derailleur arrière (rear derailleur)
pignons (rear sprocket)

pedales
(pedal)

cale-pied (toe clip)
courroie de cale-pied (toe strap)

roue dentée (chain wheel)
plateau cinq vitesses (five-speed front plate)
double plateaux (ten-speed front plate)

bequille (kickstand)

La Bicyclette Francaise

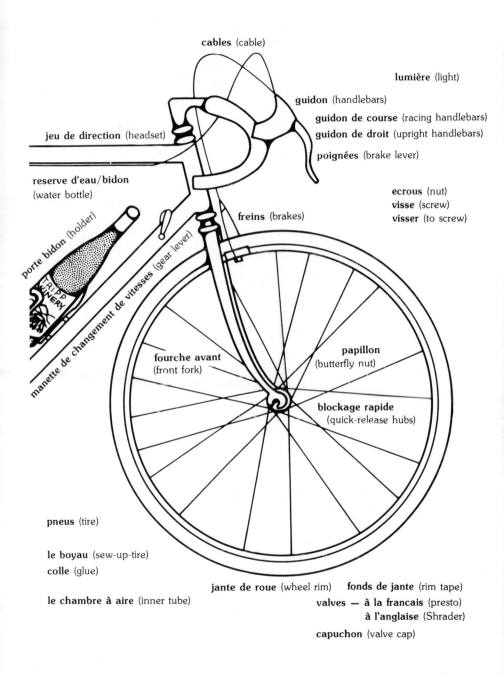

cables (cable)

lumière (light)

guidon (handlebars)

guidon de course (racing handlebars)

jeu de direction (headset)

guidon de droit (upright handlebars)

poignées (brake lever)

reserve d'eau/bidon
(water bottle)

ecrous (nut)
visse (screw)
visser (to screw)

porte bidon (holder)

freins (brakes)

manette de changement de vitesses (gear lever)

papillon
(butterfly nut)

fourche avant
(front fork)

blockage rapide
(quick-release hubs)

pneus (tire)

le boyau (sew-up-tire)

colle (glue)

jante de roue (wheel rim)   fonds de jante (rim tape)

le chambre à aire (inner tube)

valves — à la francais (presto)
à l'anglaise (Shrader)

capuchon (valve cap)

Packing Your Bicycle

Here is a spring and summertime bicycle touring list:
(You hard-core winter cyclists will have to adjust as necessary.)

CLOTHING:

1 dressy shirt and trousers(male), skirt or dress(female) for elegant evenings. (stay-pressed fabric!)
1 pair respectable shoes you can also bicycle in
1 pair walkable shoes you can also bicycle in. (bicycle shoes not recommended)
1 jacket or rain slicker or poncho
1 warm pullover (or running suit)
1 warm undershirt & legwarmers (polypro)
short, long & sleeveless t-shirts
2 pair bicyclable pants
3 underpants
2 bras (sorry, guys, this is a uni-sex list)
2 socks
biking gloves
1 something to sleep in, presentable in hallways of hotels
1 bathing suit

TOILETRIES

razor
shampoo
small soap packets (2)
deodorant
sunscreen/skin lotion
nailclippers/file
airplane slippers (for the discriminating traveler)
Alka-Seltzer® for hangovers (for the indiscriminate)
disinfectant for wounds
small sewing kit
dental floss, toothbrush, toothpaste
make-up and jewelry (for fancy places)
Q-tips
brush/comb
laundry powder
washcloth that can serve as emergency towel
packets of tissues

Packing Your Bicycle

TOOLS OF LIFE for you

sportswatch with alarm function
wax ear plugs for noisy places
scotch tape
Swiss army knife
one/two good books unrelated to wine or bikes
French/English dictionary
one wine guidebook (see "Bibliography" for recommendations)
passport
travelers' checks
business cards and/or some personal gifts for new friends
small change bag
small carrying bag for around-town walks
small radio for music and news lovers
address book for writing friends
pen
notebook (warning: all French notebooks are lined in squares or rectangles)

TOOLS OF LIFE for your bicycle

a bike lock with a combination, so you don't need a key
a wrench to fit each nut & bolt on your bike
tire-changing tools
tire repair kit
spare tire or tube
a good pump
a battery-operated headlight
water bottle (to which wine can be added)
bungie cords for holding things together

Two rear panniers and a handlebar bag should be sufficient in summer.

FOR BICYCLE CAMPING, add

a sleeping bag
a tent
a large, square plastic poncho for use as ground cover, raincoat, picnic
    table, bike cover at night, etc.
cookstove & cooking gear
front panniers to carry all this

BIBLIOGRAPHY & **RECOMMENDED READING**

AUBERGES DE JEUNESSE (Youth Hostels) FRANCE 84/85. Federation Unie des Auberges de Jeunesse, 6 rue Mesnil, 75116 Paris. 45.05.13.14.

AA Camping Guide to Europe — 1984. Automobile Association, London.

CAMPING IN FRANCE. (1984-85) Camping Club of Great Britain & Ireland, 11 Grosvenor Place, London SW1 England.

CHAMBRES D'HOTE DE FRANCE. 1986 Gite Rural de France, 35 rue Godot de Mauroy, 75009 Paris. 47.42.25.43.

CHATEAUX DE LOIRE 1984. Guide Michelin, 46 ave de Breteauil, 75341 Paris Cedex 07.

CHATEAUX HOTELS INDEPENDENT 1984. Shg. Publi-Reseau, 61230 Gace, France.

FAT MAN ON A BICYCLE. By Tom Vernon. Fontana Book, William Collins, Glasgow. 1984.

*FRENCH COUNTRY WINES** and **FRENCH FINE WINES**. By Steven Spurrier. Willow Books, Collins, London. 1984.

GASTRONOMIC ROUTES OF FRANCE, *THE WINES & SPIRITS OF FRENCH**. Food & Wine from France (SOPEXA), 24E. 21st St., NY 10010, U.S.A. (212) 477-9800. Other offices: 5757 W. Century Blvd., LA 90045 U.S.A., (213) 641-9145; Nuffield House, 41-46 Piccadilly, London WIV 9AJ, England, (0) 439-8371; Marine House, Clanwilliam Place, Dublin 2, Ireland. (1) 68 07 77.

GUIDE TO THE WINES & VINEYARDS OF FRANCE. By Alexis Lichine. Alfred A. Knopf, Inc., New York 1982.

HOSTELLERIE DU VIGNOBLE FRANCAIS 1984. Impasse de la Roseraie, 13420 Gemenos, France.

THE WORLD ATLAS OF WINE. 1985 By Hugh Johnson. Mitchell Beazley, Ltd., Mill House, 87-89 Shaftsbury Ave., London W1V 7AD, or Simon & Shuster, New York.

* carry these along with you.

Form Letter to Schedule a Visit to a Wine Cellar

Le_____198__
(date)

Monsieur le Directeur,

Je suis redevable de votre adresse au **GRAPE EXPEDITIONS IN FRANCE**.

Je vous serais oblige de me faire connaître la possibilité d'une visite de votre cave le _____ de _____, 198__, pour _____
(date)   (month)
personnes pendant ____le matin/____aprés-midi.

Serait-il possible de voir la cave et deguster vos vins à cette date?

Avec mes remerciements anticipés, veuillez agréer, Monsieur de Directeur, l'expression de mes sentiments distingués.

(Signature)

Nom _____

Adresse _____

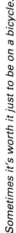

Sometimes it's worth it just to be on a bicycle.

(Enclose self-addressed, international postage-paid envelope)

Form Letter to Make
Hotel/Restaurant Reservations

Chère Madame B

Chèr madame / Monsieur

Le_____198__
  (date)

Monsieur le Directeur,

Je suis redevable de votre adresse au **GRAPE EXPEDITIONS IN FRANCE**. Je vous serais obligé de me réserver une chambre_____simple/_____double et/ou diner pour les nuits du _____ au _____.
       (arrival date)   (departure date)

Merci de me confirmer ces réservations.

Avec mes remerciements anticipés, veuillez agreér, Monsieur le Directeur, l'expression de mes sentiments distingués.

(Signature)

Nom _____

Adresse _____

(Enclose self-addressed, international postage-paid envelope.)

Index

Index

ORDER FORM

For Your Bicycling & Wine-Loving Friends:

Two great bicycle guides to the world's finest wine country:

☐ **Grape Expeditions in France** @$9.00 $_____
☐ **Grape Expeditions in** @$6.50 $_____
California (64 pages, 15 rides)
(Californians, please includes 6% sales Tax $ _____)
Postage and handling. $1.00

TOTAL $ _____

Please enclose payment to: Sally Taylor & Friends, 1442 Willard Street, San Francisco CA 94117 U.S.A. or 110 Blvd. Malesherbes, 75017 Paris, France.

SHIP TO: _____

_____
_____ Zip _____

☐ Bill with shipment (on orders over $20.)

ORDER FORM

For Your Bicycling & Wine-Loving Friends:

Two great bicycle guides to the world's finest wine country:

☐ **Grape Expeditions in France** @$9.00 $_____
☐ **Grape Expeditions in** @$6.50 $_____
California (64 pages, 15 rides)
(Californians, please includes 6% sales Tax $ _____)
Postage and handling. $1.00

TOTAL $ _____

Please enclose payment to: Sally Taylor & Friends, 1442 Willard Street, San Francisco CA 94117 U.S.A. or 110 Blvd. Malesherbes, 75017 Paris, France.

SHIP TO: _____

_____
_____ Zip _____

☐ Bill with shipment (on orders over $20.)

Stamp

POST CARD

Sally Taylor & Friends
1442 Willard Street
San Francisco CA 94117 USA

Stamp

POST CARD

Sally Taylor & Friends
1442 Willard Street
San Francisco CA 94117 USA

Bicycles and Wine in Paris

All trains and planes start from Paris, and the city itself is bicyclable, for those experienced in city cycling. Flying into Paris with a bicycle here's how to get into town:

At **CHARLES DE GAULLE AIRPORT**, the train *SNCF-RER* is about 2 km. from the airport terminals, in the basement of a tall hotel services building standing alone. The RER allows bicycles for 24 francs extra. You can carry it on. The last car usually has ceiling hooks specifically for bikes (thoughtful French Rail System).

At **ORLY** AIRPORT, the best way to get a bicycle into town is to ride it. About 10 kms. Follow the signs.

For **BICYCLE REPAIRS AND SALES** in Paris, use:

La Maison du Velo
8 rue de Belzunce
75010 Paris

Metro: Gare du Nord
(Sunday & Monday)
42.81.24.72

Francis Kelsall, the owner, is an Englishman. He sells and services touring bikes. Send him measurements, and your price range, if you want a bike waiting for your arrival. Allow 3 months.

Touring the **WINE BARS** of Paris is a great way to get introduced to the wines of France.

To **BUY WINE** to take home, use Cave LeGrand (42.60.07.12) or Steven Spurrier (42.65.92.40), but remember you have a limited ability to carry bottles on the plane. Six is about all that will fit under your seat.

For more information on the wine regions, visit:
Maison du Vin de France
21 rue Francoise 1er
75008 Paris

Metro: Roosevelt

47.20.20.76.

FOR TOURS:		LEAVE FROM:
1-3	Loire Valley	Gare d'Austerlitz
4-6	Bordeaux	Gare d'Austerlitz
7	Provence	Gare de Lyon (TGV to Marseilles/Toulon)
8	Cotes de Rhone	Gare de Lyon (TGV)
9-11	Burgundy	Gare de Lyon (TGV)
12	Champagne	Gare de l'Est

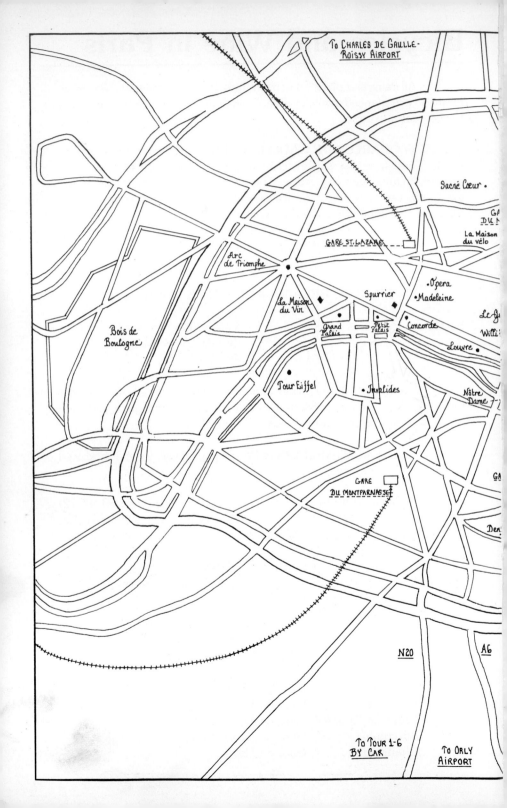